BREAKFAST
for the
HEART
*Meditations to
Nourish Your Soul*

Also by Diane M. Komp, M.D.

A Window to Heaven
A Child Shall Lead Them
Hope Springs from Mended Places
Images of Grace

BREAKFAST

for the

HEART

Meditations to
Nourish Your Soul

DIANE M. KOMP, M.D.

ZondervanPublishingHouse
Grand Rapids, Michigan

A Division of HarperCollinsPublishers

Breakfast for the Heart
Copyright © 1996 by Diane M. Komp

Requests for information should be addressed to:

🏛 ZondervanPublishingHouse
Grand Rapids, Michigan 49530

Library of Congress Cataloging-in-Publication Data

Komp, Diane M.
    Breakfast for the heart : meditations to nourish your soul / Diane M. Komp.
        p.   cm.
    Includes bibliographical references.
    ISBN: 0-310-20916-1 (hardcover : alk. paper)
    1. Meditations.   2. Devotional calendars. I. Title.
BV4811.K67   1996
242'.2—dc20   96–16554
                                              CIP

This edition printed on acid-free paper and meets the American National Standards Institute Z39.48 standard.

Parts of this book first appeared in *Daily Guideposts* and are reprinted here with permission from *Daily Guideposts 1994, 1995,* and *1996,* © 1993, 1994, 1995 by Guideposts Associates, Inc., Carmel, N.Y. 10512. Quotations from the Bible include the King James Version (KJV); the New Revised Standard Version (NRSV), © 1990 by the National Council of Churches of Christ in the United States of America; the Revised Standard Version (RSV), © 1946, 1952, 1971 by the Division of Christian Education of the National Council of Churches of Christ in the United States of America; the New International Version (NIV), © 1973, 1978, 1984 by the International Bible Society; the Jerusalem Bible (JB), © 1966, 1967, 1968 by Dartman, Longman & Todd, Ltd., and Doubleday & Co., Inc., and J. B. Phillips (JBP), © 1947, 1952, 1955, 1957 as *The Gospels* and *Letters to Young Churches* by The Macmillan Company. The African prayers referred to in "Tasting the Bread of Life" are taken from *With All God's People: The New Ecumenical Prayer Cycle* compiled by John Cardeu for the World Council of Churches, Geneva 1989. Portions of "Jenny's Mommy" appeared first in *Theology Today* (XLVI: 411–419, 1990) © Diane M. Komp. Portions of "An Irish Rascal" appeared first as "Welcome Back to the Wonderful World of Thermo" in the Houghton College *Milieu*, 1985. Portions of "A Lowly Association" appeared in *All God's Creatures,* © by Guideposts Associates, Inc.

Edited by Lori J. Walburg
Interior design by Sue Vandenberg Koppenol

Printed in the United States of America

---

97 98 99 00 01 02 03/❖ QF/ 10 9 8 7 6 5 4

CONTENTS

4
LOOK IT UP IN YOUR HEART

5
GENTLE COMPANIONS

6
BETWEEN A ROCK AND A HARD PLACE

10
A GERMAN ATTIC

11
FEAR NO EVIL

12
WEEDS INTO WILDFLOWERS

Begin the day with Christ and prayer—you need no other. Creedless, with it you have religion; creedstuffed, it will leaven any theological dough in which you stick . . . Learn to know your Bible. In forming character and in shaping conduct, its touch has still its ancient power.

Sir William Osler
at Yale University

FROM MY HEART TO YOURS

We are adhering to life now with our last muscle—the heart.

Djuna Barnes

I have some encouraging words for those of you who are hanging onto life by your heartstrings:

Set yourself down in your favorite easy chair.

Pour yourself that first morning cup of coffee.

Relax and read on *if you're ready for a change of heart.*

No, it's not a medical prescription I have to offer. I have in mind a spiritual adventure. For the next twelve weeks I want to show you that the Bible is not only *for* you, it is *about* you. Your life story is so important that God thought of it first. But God is not finished with your story yet. And you have a part in how that story turns out.

To help you find yourself in the Bible's pages and illustrate the process I'm talking about, I'll share some stories from my own life. You'll find daily devotionals in this book, grouped in sections of five. Each of the sixty pieces begins with a Scripture verse and is followed by an application that I've called a *heartbeat.*

I suggest that you use these readings Monday through Friday and take a break for the weekend, the same way you rest from your work. There is space right in this book for you to journal about your reactions to the heartbeats, much the way an electrocardiogram makes a tracing of our physical heart's activity.

My guess is that you will have much to think and write about. So did I as I wrote this book. Let me refresh my opening invitation:

Tuck your feet up under you so you're cozy.

Warm up your coffee before it gets too cold.

Breathe easy, and above all else, take heart, *for everything that was written in the past was written to teach us, so that through endurance and the encouragement of the Scriptures we might have hope* (Romans 15:4 NIV).

Diane M. Komp, M.D.
March 1996

1

THE BREAKFAST OF CHAMPIONS

Everyone who competes in the games goes into strict training.

1 Corinthians 9:25 NIV

1

BREAKFAST FOR THE HEART

*Jesus said to them, "Come and have break-
fast."*

John 21:12 NIV

There's a saying in German that stands in sharp contrast to modern American eating habits: "Eat the supper of a pauper, the midday
meal of a burgher, and the breakfast of a king." This alimentary advice
is a sensible path to a peaceful night's sleep. I like to wake up early in
the morning, refreshed and ready for the day.

I digest more than my physical nourishment early in the day. My
morning begins alone with God, a breakfast for my heart. If I intend
to find peaceful moments at a later hour, it never happens. My mind
becomes busy with too many other things. At bedtime I'm usually too
tired to concentrate on what God may want to say.

When I was a young doctor, I closed the Bible and turned my
back on the Christian faith I had professed in my youth. As I saw the
suffering of my patients, I could no longer believe that there was a
God who cared about our world. Early in this "conversion to disbelief,"
I dismissed Christianity's favorite Book as irrelevant to my life. Some
fifteen years later I reconsidered those conclusions.*

This second time around, I examined the Bible critically, the
way I would approach any book. I wanted to be convinced that I
should pay attention. I didn't feel obliged to believe a word I read. One

quiet morning I heard God speaking through its pages. I'm still listening today.

In the woods that surround my home, baby robins warm up their warbles just prior to dawn. Sunrise filters through the hemlocks and pries open my eyes. In these moments of peace with the world, God invites me to break my fast. He feeds me with his Word, just as Jesus once fed some fisherfolk by the Tiberias Sea. Before the cares of the day have a chance to drown out his voice, I give God a chance to speak. "Di, do you love me?" he often asks.

When this breakfast for my heart is complete, as I get ready for my work, God sends me off with instructions for the day: "Di," he says, "feed my other sheep."

🕭 HEARTBEAT: *Write an appointment in your calendar for a "breakfast for the heart" with God for tomorrow morning. Make notes about what you hope will happen at your breakfast meeting.*

> — to have him help me
> become less anxious over
> things that I cannot control.
> — to have him help me in
> the next chapter of life.

---

*This story is told in my book *A Window to Heaven: When Children See Life in Death* (Grand Rapids: Zondervan, 1992).

2

ABSENT WITHOUT THE LORD

Why did you despise the word of the LORD by doing what is evil in his eyes?

2 Samuel 12:9 NIV

My crisis of faith is an experience that more than doctors live through. *If there is no justice in the universe*, I reasoned, *there cannot be a God. If there is no loving God, what use is a god at all?* These were my first steps in going "AWOL"—Absent Without the Lord.

In the void that followed, I discarded the Bible. I concluded that I had to decide what was right and wrong. I trusted my own judgment about my life and my career in medicine.

Many years later, a medical student asked me a question. He wanted to be like me—his professor. Wondering what had been the greatest goal in my medical career, he asked (with certainty), "To find a cure for cancer?" Surely that must have been the case.

My heart filled with a suffocating darkness when I heard his assumption. If I had answered him honestly, I would have told him that my goal was to *treat* cancer rather than to cure it. With a *cure* for cancer, there seemed nothing left for me to do with my life. As I heard myself talking within my heart, I became alarmed. At some subconscious level, I wanted cancer to continue to exist! With notions like this, how could I trust my own judgment?

I stammered out some answer to the student, then excused myself so my young friend could disturb my thoughts no more. But his question and the dis-ease it created remained for many years until I finally invited God back into my life.

Today, that student is a fine doctor with great gifts of healing. I thank him for his question, for it showed me the terrible price I was paying for despising the Word of God.

🌱 HEARTBEAT: *Recall an incident where God used someone in the present to remind you of a truth that you learned when you were much younger.*

Mom is always reminding me of what it means to have truth.

The she told me the other morning that she had to go to meeting because that is what helped her get through the rest of the week.

3

HOLY HEARTBURN

Did not our heart burn within us, while he talked with us by the way, and while he opened to us the scriptures?

Luke 24:32 KJV

Back in the days when I was a church-going kid, I memorized so many Bible verses that I won contests. By the time I became a doctor, I had substituted facts that were supposed to save lives.

One day at the hospital, I had no medicine or words of consolation to offer seven-year-old Anna.* I asked a nurse to remove unneeded medical equipment from her room and sat there quietly in the darkened room with the dying child and her parents.

At the moment of her death, Anna saw and heard angels. Her pale face was transformed by perfect peace. *Let not your hearts be troubled,* I heard. Where did those words come from? *My peace I give to you, not as the world gives.*

In the quiet of my heart, I heard the Word (from John 14:1, 27). In *my* heart—so near! In medical school I learned to suppress my feelings about my patients, but God had never removed his Word from my heart. It was all there, stored up for the time when I could hear with more than my ears.

Perhaps that was what happened on the road to Emmaus. The disciples knew *in their heads* what the Scriptures foretold about the

Messiah. But it wasn't until Jesus applied it *to their hearts* that they recognized him for who he really was.

Today I go through the Bible and note the hundreds of verses I learned as a child. I write them on cards to refresh my memory. And then I sit back in a quiet place, stripped of distractions—and listen.

☞ HEARTBEAT: *Choose a Bible verse you memorized at an earlier time in your life and relearn it in a different translation or a foreign language. If you've never memorized Scripture before, start by learning Luke 24:32.*

7/9/12

Psalm 118 - This is the day which the Lord hath made, we will rejoice & be glad in it.

---

*I've changed some names and minor details throughout this book to protect privacy and confidentiality.

4

BURIED TREASURE

I have treasured your promises in my heart,
since I have no wish to sin against you.

Psalm 119:11 JB

My first prayer to God after fifteen years of silence was delivered with what I can only describe as *chutzpah.* First, I challenged God as to what the new rules for our relationship were going to be. "You don't have any of me now," I prayed, "so you should be pleased with anything I offer you." Then I started to read the Bible, as I said before—like any other book. Since I was starting from a basis of total disbelief, I didn't have to believe anything I read.

Starting with the gospel of Luke, I read: "Therefore, since I myself have carefully investigated everything from the beginning, it seemed good also to me to write an orderly account for you" (Luke 1:3). *Remarkable!* I thought. Luke's "orderly account" was written the way I'd expect a physician to report. Methodically. Carefully. What followed Luke's introduction were stories about the healing of sick people, written in clinical detail. I was fascinated. I couldn't wait to wake up each morning at 5:30 to read more.

Somewhere within the first two weeks, God's Word started to get a hold on me. As I finished Luke's account of Jesus and his subsequent book about the apostles, I was intrigued by this ancient doctor who continued to practice medicine after he embarked on his spiritual adventure. Thanks to Dr. Luke, God's Word reactivated in my heart.

I don't tell you this story to recommend either my opening prayer or my path back to putting my life into God's hands. But did you notice how loving and patient God is and how powerful is his Word?

☞ HEARTBEAT: *Write out a prayer that expresses all the doubts you have. Come back to that prayer when you finish this book and strike through the doubts that have disappeared.*

5

THE FLAKING TOTEM POLE

What use is an idol once its maker has shaped it—a cast image, a teacher of lies? For its maker trusts in what has been made, though the product is only an idol that cannot speak!

Habakkuk 2:18 NRSV

My Jesus, I love thee. I know thou art mine. "Love you?" I thought. "Why, I hardly know you!" I was paying careful attention to the hymns I sang when I started to attend church again. (I warned you I wasn't planning to give God an easy time!) Since I had not only memorized a lot of Scripture, but also *all* the verses of *all* the old hymns, I avoided reeling out the words from rote memory. "But I want to know God!" I pleaded.

I left that church service with an attitude of prayer that went with me the whole week. One morning when I was early for an appointment, I passed the time sitting in my car praying. As I prayed, an image came to me of an old weather-beaten totem pole. The original colors were hidden beneath layers of peeling paint. Restoring the authentic design would require getting rid of the obscuring coats of color. But I was willing to invest the effort, for I really wanted to know what was underneath.

During this prayer I realized that the God I thought I knew as a child, but abandoned as a young doctor, was an idol constructed of my own misconceptions of who God is. It was time to recognize all the mortals I had allowed to represent God for me. So many different faces! Eventually, each of them—parents, pastors, professors—had failed to measure up. In my mind, God had failed to measure up as well.

None of these people meant to become gods. They simply meant to guide. I had chosen to idolize humans who were destined to fail. In that moment of prayer, I recognized that I had another choice: I could peel away the flaking paint to find God and love him for who he is.

🐝 HEARTBEAT: *Identify something in your life that has taken God's place in your life and put it back in its proper place.*

7/13/12 → Friday!

-I would say that out the simple little metal box known as a T.V. has to many different idols that I have admired but has taken time away from God.
-Some of my friends also.
-Perhaps my dad too.

2
BLESSED ARE
THE HOMESICK

Blessed are the homesick, for they shall journey home.

Jung-Stilling

1

WILD TURKEYS
AND WITCH'S BROOMS

We know that the whole creation has been groaning in labor pains until now.

Romans 8:22 NRSV

To get to my home in Connecticut, I drive along a winding back road lined with stone walls and casual country gardens. One of my neighbors spent the entire summer planting a new border of flowering shrubs. Shortly thereafter, one of his bright little bushes—a witch's broom—disappeared.

A family of wild turkeys has moved into our woods a little farther down the road. On pleasant days there's a hen who thinks nothing of sitting down in the middle of the road to enjoy a sunbath. The first time I saw her yawn at me, I was driving faster than I should have been and nearly ran down her droopy eyelids.

Two endangered species in less than a mile of Moose Hill Road—but a situation full of hope. The gardener replaced the witch's broom and planted a large, clearly worded sign: *SHAME ON YOU*. Two weeks have passed and his garden remains inviolate. The turkey-lady is still out there strutting and sunning. She has not changed her ways at all, but I have mended mine. I'm more careful to obey the posted speed limit on our country road.

The missing witch's broom and the prancing turkey hen remind me that reverence and respect for creation begin on country roads where plants and wild turkeys groan and wait for God's children to take action one at a time.

🖤 HEARTBEAT: *Look around your neighborhood. Adopt a representative of God's creation that you need to treat with more respect.*

= The grass on Middle Earth.
= Our flowers in this heat.
- The trees that are needing to be cut down due to dead branches etc.
- My two wonderful neighbors, Bobbee & Gracie. Need to visit more w/ them.

2

PURSUITS WITH ROOTS

*Every plant which my Heavenly Father did
not plant will be pulled up by the roots.*

Matthew 15:13 JBP

For many years I enjoyed the passionate pursuit of growing orchids. I built a greenhouse for my collection and was always on the lookout for new friends who shared the same obsession. There's a name for that process of visiting other orchid fanatics—to "go orchiding."

To go orchiding is to learn that not just people have generations worthy of consideration. Let me tell you how really quaint orchid fanciers are. When we go orchiding, we have been known to *ooh* and *aah* over plain green leaves of tiny seedlings that have not yet come into bloom. To an orchid nut, the unpretentious leaves hint about the future.

Without reference to labels or records, a true orchid maven knows each valued plant's parentage. To imagine what is yet to be, you listen to the recitation of the generations that came before. The botanical lineage predicts shape, form, and color of future flowers. If a plant is not true to its heritage, I will relegate it to a back bench when it blooms. Even its price depends on who its parents are and how faithfully its potential is realized.

These baby orchid plants remind me of what it means to be my heavenly Father's offspring, even on those days when nothing beautiful is apparent in my life. Knowing who my Father is defines my potential. I have been "born from above" to display my new parentage in my life.

❦ HEARTBEAT: *Identify an area of your life where your heavenly parentage shows.*

- In my husband & kids.

3

A HOUSE FULL OF DREAMS

*Have a reputation for being reasonable, and
never forget the nearness of your Lord.*
Philippians 4:5 JBP

My Connecticut hideaway fills me with serenity. This home is
truly a place where I can let God speak to me. My house is very con-
temporary, and my bedroom is almost in the trees. It seems fitting that
the place I do my dreaming is so close to the heavens.

Sometimes I write my dreams down in my journal, even if I don't
understand what a particular dream means at the time. I notice that
my home is a prominent part of this New England reverie. As I
browsed through my journal one day, I realized that in my dreams,
my house represents me.

One time I dreamed that I.was in the garden looking at the border of my property. The grass was hedged in by a neat, tight row of
tough, attractive pachysandra. Then I looked again, and the pachys
were gone, replaced by tender vines of perennial periwinkle. The periwinkle (Vinca) seemed more vulnerable than the pachy, but there was
a serene strength and solidity in the soft carpet of blue and white
flowers. I remembered that one of the most important drugs to cure
cancer comes from a Vinca vine. As tender as the vine may appear, it
offers healing to many precious children in my hospital.

The interpretation of the dream was not apparent that night, but I realized later that this is exactly what God is doing in my life. At Yale I move and shake with some of the most powerful figures in academic medicine today. I find it hard to interact with some of my esteemed colleagues without putting up a shield to keep some of my fellow movershakers at a protective distance. In contrast, the very act of writing about my spiritual life—letting the whole world know what is happening in my soul—leaves me feeling very vulnerable.

God is taking away my impenetrable border, even if I would prefer to have it surrounding me. He's replacing it with something gentler but more powerful. Through the process of writing, I have found it easier to share this fragile side of myself. Surprisingly, some of my friends at Yale share deeply from their own souls after they read my books.

The pachy and the periwinkle tell the story of the healing that continues in my soul. Wouldn't you like to use the journal space that follows to tell about the healing that is happening in your own life?

HEARTBEAT: *Note some area of your life where you need to risk being vulnerable if God is to do his work through you.*

7/13/12

This coming year...

what do I DO!

4

UNDER CONSTRUCTION

By wisdom a house is built, and through understanding it is established; through knowledge its rooms are filled with rare and beautiful treasures.

Proverbs 24:3 NIV

I was standing in my house looking up when a catastrophe started to happen. The cathedral ceiling started to buckle. Plaster fell, hitting my head. I ran for my life. Standing outside, I watched as my beautiful house crumbled and fell. Last year I invested thousands of dollars in repairs, but it had not been enough!

The cave-in destroyed everything I owned and valued: my crystal, my china, my paintings—even my beloved books. All my savings were in this house. Better that this happened now, I thought, when I am simplifying my lifestyle and giving more to others. Somehow, the loss of my possessions did not seem as great as it would have a few years ago.

I thought for certain that the insurance company would declare the house a total loss. Instead, they sent workers to rebuild the structure. I walked through the first room that the builder was completing. Curiously, he didn't even consult me about the original design of the house as his work progressed. The contractor was rebuilding the house according to a new plan of his own choice.

I had to admit that the new house was a better one than the old. This master carpenter had allowed the natural beauty of the outdoors to come into the living area and complement the room. His helpers were finishing the walls on a second room when I walked through. There were shelves full of books by Henri Nouwen, an author whose spiritual writings mean much to me. Even my new library was better than the one I had lost.

At that point I woke up and realized that all of this was a dream. My heart was pounding, but as I thought about the powerful imagery of the dream, my breathing slowed down. I had met this Carpenter in dreams before. Usually he appears, without being summoned, just when I am hard at work planning my own life. I fell back to sleep remembering that Jesus asks me to forsake my plans to follow his. There's nothing I've built that can begin to compare with his plans for my life.

☞ HEARTBEAT: *What might need to be "destroyed" in your life so that Jesus can finish building you by his far better plan?*

5

THE KOMP-ENDIUM

His mercy is on those who fear him from generation to generation.

Luke 1:50 RSV

For years I've been researching my family tree. When I rummage through ancient graveyards, I feel like I'm a character in a grand mystery story. Something dynamic is happening in my family that has never died and never will.

One of my great-great-grandfathers, Samuel Pupplett Carr, came from Colchester, England. I found the Carr headstones in a churchyard near the eighteenth-century family home. The vicar of that church graciously invited me into his vestry. He pointed to a framed silhouette on the wall of Samuel Pupplett Carr's uncle, one of his predecessors. The next day he introduced me to one of my living distant cousins who was also a vicar in Colchester.

Cousin Eric recited a fascinating saga of Flemish Huguenots exiled to Essex during the Reformation for the sake of "Gottes Worde." There were persecuted Quakers in the family bloodline as well. Years later, I found the cornfields in Indiana that overshadowed the last resting place of Heinrich and Elisabetha Komp. Reading through a mid-nineteenth-century German newspaper from the tiny Indiana farm town, I learned that one of the Komp sons became a circuit-riding preacher. Another son, my great-grandfather, married Mr.

Carr's daughter, bringing the English and German sides of the family together.

So much of what I hear and read about family life today is described in terms of "dysfunction." Our society has substituted social workers for grandmothers and psychotherapists for priests. Instead of listening to narratives that link our stories with the past, we focus inward as if our own stories eclipse all others. But I'm convinced that we can break the power of skeletons from the past if we dig for the blessings from generation to generation, name them, and remember.

Today not everyone in my family is a believer. For many years, neither was I. I've written down the heritage we share in what I call our "Komp-endium." When they are ready, all my relatives can read there of the mercies of the Lord.

In my family, mercy moves from generation to generation. I suspect it does in yours as well, even if you have to dig deep to find it.

☞ HEARTBEAT: *Dig in your family history for some evidence of God's working in your family's story.*

3
WISE INSTRUCTION

A teacher affects eternity.
Henry Adams

1

A FATHER'S WORDS

*Hear, my child, your father's instruction . . . if
sinners entice you, do not consent.*

Proverbs 1:8, 10 NRSV

Like most teenagers, I had more than a few missed curfews to
my credit (or debit, depending on your point of view). These recol-
lections return as vivid memories when I think back on my father's
earliest instructions. Now I see Dad's rules and regs in quite a different light than I did at the time.

One Sunday evening after a church youth group meeting, I
lounged too long at a local ice cream parlor, enjoying my friends' company. I was chin deep in a three-scoop hot fudge sundae when my
father appeared at the establishment door, scowling and silent. *I
knew that look!* I was mortified, and made the fatal mistake of ques-
tioning his standard. How could he ask more from me than these fine
Christian parents who didn't mind if their kids were out this late?

Dad had his own way to deal with holier-than-thou adolescence.
Stony silence. The last words I heard from him that evening were:
"Tomorrow is a school day." I feared my father most when he had noth-
ing to say, and nothing was said for the ten city blocks we walked home.

Today, the teenager who once lost track of time so easily now has
a built-in clock for time. I am prized and praised in my adult life for
my punctuality. When I visited Dad in the final years of his life, we

often sat in silence. But there were also times when he had something brief to say, like: "Di, I love you," or, "Di, I'm so proud of you."

As a teen I remember fearing my father's stern judgment. I remember him fearing for my safety in New York City, as well. But in those last years we had tears, not fear, in both of our eyes. I returned his favor and told Dad how proud I was that he was my dad.

❦ HEARTBEAT: *Recall a wise instruction that God gave you through your earthly dad.*

_____

_____

_____

_____

_____

_____

_____

_____

_____

_____

_____

_____

_____

_____

2

A PROVERBIAL TEACHER

*Besides being wise, the Teacher also taught
the people knowledge, weighing and studying
and arranging many proverbs.*

Ecclesiastes 12:9 NRSV

My high school years were more than church youth groups and ice cream. I thrived on my science and math courses, and I soon found myself seriously considering a career in medicine. Teachers of biology, chemistry, and physics filled my head full of the sort of stuff that I thought I needed to make my way in the world.

One of my teachers—not in the sciences—found my head too stuffed with stuff. She was my senior English teacher for an advanced placement college course. Mrs. Siegel weighed and studied and decided that some of my proverbs needed rearranging.

So careful and precise was she about the words she used, that I remember the shape of her mouth and the shade of her lipstick. Unimpressed with the young scientist before her, she tossed me a challenge—right in class. "Why are you going to college?" she asked me.

"To become a doctor," was my confident reply.

"Wrong!" she lamented. Her lips pursed. "Try again."

"To *learn how* to become a doctor?" I proposed in a more tentative tone.

"No," she shook her head, "you haven't gotten it yet. I had hoped you would go to college to learn how to become a human being who happens to be a doctor."

Long ago I forgot the names of my high school science teachers, as excellent as they might have been. I've also forgotten most of those trivial facts that once filled my head. But I still remember Mrs. Siegel. She taught me that reading, writing, and public speaking are tools of life for us all. I can imagine her smile as I write today. When I succeed as a communicator and a simple human being, I am most able to be the doctor that my patients need me to be.

☞ HEARTBEAT: *Name a valuable gift God gave you through a teacher.*

3

A STRICT BOSS

No discipline seems pleasant at the time, but painful. Later on, however, it produces a harvest of righteousness and peace for those who have been trained by it.

Hebrews 12:11 NIV

Nathaniel "Boss" Levine was one of the strictest teachers at Midwood High School, but no one was more beloved. Because of Boss, the most important activity in our high school was music. Instead of pursuing sports, many of us added hours of sight-singing and music theory to the already rigorous daily chorus rehearsals.

None of us doubted what a serious person Boss could be. One day when we were particularly off-key in rehearsal, I saw the color rising in his face. "I can't stand this!" he exploded. With a cherubic grin he quietly added, "So I'll sit down." And he did. We laughed nervously and then sang perfectly the rest of the hour.

When I look back on our experience under Boss's baton, I realize that we *wanted* his strictness. We *allowed* him an occasional outburst. We *needed* someone with his high standards to help us form our own. I see it today with my own students.

My students today watch everything I do. This is how they learn the "art" of medicine—those personal skills that will help them see their patients as more than the diseases that brought them to a doctor.

I want my students to remember everything I say that doesn't match up to the highest standards of our profession. I want them to hold me accountable and adopt high standards for themselves. They need that vision. The strictness by which my students judge me gives me the privilege to explode from time to time for the sake of their future patients. "I can't stand this!" I may say. Then I sit down so that my students can do it over and get it right.

❦ HEARTBEAT: *Remember an episode in your life where strictness worked to your benefit.*

AN IRISH RASCAL

And the Lord's servant must not be quarrelsome but kindly to everyone, an apt teacher, forbearing.

2 Timothy 2:24 RSV

As useful as all those high school liberal arts courses have proven, my success in college ultimately boiled down to how I would fare in one dreaded course—physical chemistry. The upper-class chemistry majors added fire to freshman fear as they enveloped the course description in mystery and mythology. They never explained why "P. Chem." was so difficult. It simply was, they intoned. The college catalogue was more neutral in its description of the class, but hardly a source of comfort.

In contrast to the more popular majors, only four of us were the lone survivors in the chemistry major. We dreaded the first exam our senior year and held our collective breath as Professor Fred Shannon bounced into the classroom. He handed out the test booklets. "Welcome to the wonderful world of Thermo!" we read.

Professor Shannon, whom I must describe as a red-headed Irish rascal, had woven his questions on the laws of thermodynamics into the mythical adventures of a superhero he named "Thermo." We smiled. We relaxed. We plodded through the exam in peace. Professor Shannon had his own way to get us over our fear of the subject.

I am a teacher now myself. Although not as witty and patient as Fred Shannon, I learned from him that consideration for my students is just as important as focusing on my subject. Fear is a poor teacher. On the other hand, humor and understanding put everyone—not just students—at ease.

❧ HEARTBEAT: *Take a situation today where someone might be afraid. Through your words and actions turn it into an experience of hospitality for that person.*

5

A PATIENT CUBAN

Let patience have her perfect work.
James 1:4 KJV

In medical school, I met another most unusual mentor. Until Fidel Castro took over Cuba, Dr. Torres had been a prominent professor of cardiology in the island nation.

After he fled with his family to America for refuge, he had to start his postgraduate training all over again to be licensed here to practice medicine. When I met him, he was a lowly hospital resident.

Although he was older than the other residents, Dr. Torres seemed to have more energy than the rest of them combined.One night when I was on duty, I watched an intern fuss and throw a fit. For fifteen minutes Stuart had tried and failed to place an IV needle into a tiny infant on our ward. Dr. Torres came along and took the intern's place. Silently, the older man worked for an hour before the needle slipped into a willing vein.

"Dr. Torres," Stuart confessed, "I'm so embarrassed. After a few minutes, I was cursing. But you, you stood there patiently for an hour and never said a word."

"Stuart," Torres said, putting his arm kindly around the tired younger man,"let me tell you something. After Castro, this was nothing!"

This vignette happened more than thirty years ago. I remember it as if it happened this morning because so often I come to the end of my patience. But then I reach back in my memory and find not only Dr. Torres's lesson, but all the hardships in my life that required a new level of endurance. With this expanding catalogue of inspirational examples in mind, I can do the seemingly impossible at least once a week and afterward say, "This was nothing!"

☞ HEARTBEAT: *Make note of an "impossible" task that comes your way today. The next time you face that task, repeat it with more patience.*

4
LOOK IT UP
IN YOUR HEART

*Go to your bosom; knock there, and
ask your heart what it doth know.*
William Shakespeare

1

LOOK IT UP IN YOUR HEART

I pray also that the eyes of your heart may be enlightened.

Ephesians 1:18 NIV

The child's dark complexion was a striking contrast to the blond-haired, blue-eyed couple she called "Mom" and "Dad." I know I must have been staring at the family, but I wondered what their story was. Adoption, to be sure. Eventually I had my chance to learn because Sophie opened a conversation with me. Then her proud mother wanted to tell me more.

Both Sophie and her brother were Romanian orphans whom Mom and Dad had adopted. Something in Sophie's eight-year-old self-confidence caught my attention and held it, so I asked my burning question.

"Do you know how special it is to be chosen?" I probed. Sophie nodded quickly, a bit too fast, I thought. I pressed her again, "But how do you *really* know how special it is to be chosen by your mom and dad?"

Sophie smiled at me. Then she shook her head, a little in wonder, a lot in amazement that I didn't comprehend. "Why, Di!" she said to me. "I know that because I looked it up in my heart."

I see that little smiling face before me as I write this story for you. I'm thinking about all the things that I know that I really need to *know.* And I recall how often it has been a child who finally taught me how to take the things that I learned with my head and prove them with my heart so that they can truly be mine.

❦ HEARTBEAT: *Name something that you know for certain because you learned it from a child.*

_____

_____

_____

_____

_____

_____

_____

_____

_____

_____

_____

_____

_____

_____

2

A CHARLIE BROWN MOMENT

*[Jesus said:] "Just as you did it to one of the
least of these who are members of my family,
you did it to me."*

Matthew 25:40 NRSV

It was a Charlie Brown moment from which only Snoopy and Lucy were missing. In the door frame before me stood a little curly-haired girl with eyes like saucers, dressed in violet bib overalls. Her name was Franny. I learned from her uplifted hand that she was four fingers old, exactly the same age as my friends' son, Justin.

Justin raced around the room, shrieking and ignoring his same-sized guest. Finally, his mother gave Justin his marching orders, and he sulked off to play with Franny. A few minutes later, Justin reappeared in the living room where I was reading.

"I'm lonely," he said.

"How can you be lonely?" I inquired. "You have a guest."

"She wants to play house," he complained. "Franny *always* wants to play house." Justin climbed onto my lap, hoping to escape whatever domestic chores the little curly-haired girl had in mind.

"You're the host," I reminded him. "That means you have certain responsibilities."

"I don't *want* to play house," Justin whined.

"What would you do," I wondered out loud for the sake of my little friend, "if Jesus came to the front door and asked you to play house with him?"

Justin molded to my bosom and thought for a long time. He rolled his eyes around in search of the right answer. "I'd play house with Jesus," he finally had to admit.

Jesus said that he will come to us in the form of people we least expect. For Justin, the little curly-haired girl was the last person he expected to bring Jesus into his private world. After one last deep sigh, Justin relinquished his comfortable position and climbed down off my lap. As he returned to his playmate, I sighed deeply myself because I'm certain that Jesus will come to me tomorrow in a way that I can hardly begin to imagine. Jesus will find some simple way to stir me out of my own biases.

☞ HEARTBEAT: *Look for an unlikely member of Jesus' family today. How does Jesus show himself to you through that person?*

3

A GOLDEN GIFTER

So always treat others as you would like them to treat you.

Matthew 7:12 JB

"Mommy! Daddy! Chrissie!"

Crumb Bunny* woke up from her nap and called half-sleepily from her bedroom. Her parents, Sue and Barry, were hosting someone important enough that her name came from their child's lips when she first awoke. Chrissie had traveled all the way from England to visit the family. What a privilege it was to meet the woman whose bone marrow donation had saved Crumb Bunny's life a little more than a year before!

Without this lovely young mother from Buckinghamshire, Crumb Bunny would have died from the same rare disease that claimed the life of her brother. But Crumb Bunny was alive and would live!

A special relationship had developed between my little patient and her benefactor. A few days earlier, they met for the first time. At a press conference at Yale, Crumb Bunny climbed up onto Chrissie's lap and received a gentle kiss on the forehead. The journalists all held their breath.

On the eleven o'clock news that night, the anchorpersons had difficulty maintaining their composure when the camera froze on that simple maternal gesture. What sort of modern woman was this? "Why did you become a bone marrow donor?" they asked Chrissie.

Blushing in a way that complemented her auburn hair, Chrissie replied, "I have three children of my own. If one of my children needed a bone marrow transplantation, I hope someone would care about them."

This was the first time that I heard someone in my hospital explain the Golden Rule through her own life—and on national television!

I know that Chrissie's words were from the heart and not calculated. But her modest declaration was far more effective than any planned campaign to recruit bone marrow donors. People called the hospital all evening to learn how they could save the life of another little Crumb Bunny.**

☞ HEARTBEAT: *Capture a golden moment today when your obedience to God brings new life to someone you meet.*

---

*The story of Crumb Bunny's successful bone marrow transplantation is told in "A Child Shall Lead Them" in *Images of Grace: A Pediatrician's Trilogy of Faith, Hope, and Love* (Grand Rapids: Zondervan, 1996). She is now a happy, healthy six-year-old who has never shown any evidence of recurrence of the disease that once threatened to take her life.

**For more information about becoming a bone marrow donor, contact the National Bone Marrow Donor Program at 1-800-MARROW2.

4

JENNY'S MOMMY

[Jesus said:] "I am the Root and the Offspring of David."

Revelation 22:16 NIV

I didn't know any of my neighbors when my dog, Jenny, and I moved from the "y'all-come-by-and-see-us-sometime" South to "don't-speak-until-you're-spoken-to" New England. Because of busy days at the hospital, I didn't have much time to go around and introduce myself. Jenny took care of that for me, for even in Yankeeland, my dog had no trouble establishing contact with total strangers.

Starting at backyard barbecues, Jenny found scores of little children whom she could train to feed her hot dogs straight from the grill. My dog, who looked like a miniature Old English sheepdog, became one of the children's best little friends. From their backyards, Jenny moved into their various homes. Poised and dancing on her hind legs before high chairs, her grateful mouth open, Jenny waited for an offering. Sometimes she crawled into little neighbor beds at nap time. Children loved to rub their faces in her silky hair. The dog and the children hid their secret under the blankets where they snuggled together until giggles betrayed their common plot.

Somehow Jenny told the children all about her family. Whenever I walked on our street, the children would greet me: "Huwo, Jenny's mommy!" My name wasn't important. What I did for a living was totally trivial. The children only cared whose mother I was.

There are moments of vanity when I think about my accomplishments as doctor and writer. King David, monarch and poet, must have had moments like these as well. But I'm reminded that I know King David best, not for his own accomplishments, but for his "root and offspring"—Jesus Christ. David's story is complete only when I hear it as part of the greater story that issued from it. I pray that the same will happen to me as my life's story unfolds.

❦ HEARTBEAT: *Name something important that has developed from your life. Why is your "issue" greater than anything for which you yourself will be remembered?*

_____

_____

_____

_____

_____

_____

_____

_____

_____

_____

_____

5

GRANDMA AND GRANDPA

Remember the days of old; consider the generations long past. Ask your father and he will tell you, your elders, and they will explain to you.
Deuteronomy 32:7 NIV

"Grandma" wistfully sips from a perfect bone china teacup. "Grandpa" looks serious in his lounge jacket as he reads the *Staatszeitung*. During my childhood they lived on a high shelf out of little children's reach. "Be careful," my mother would warn my sister and me about her prize porcelain possessions. "Grandma and Grandpa came from Germany many years ago. They can never be replaced."

After my mother's death, I researched our family tree. I started with a handwritten genealogy I found in Daddy's desk. Unlike Mom, Dad didn't understand my fascination with such old things. In some ways, more of Grandma and Grandpa lives on in me than in him.

Grandma and Grandpa Komp never taught their children to speak German. Instead, they used the language to hold private conversations behind their children's backs. For many years Dad denied knowing more than basic tourist words he had learned on business trips. Then he had a stroke, and something changed. He heard me talking to someone in German one day and understood everything I said. I smiled to myself, wondering what my grandparents thought they had kept secret from Dad and my two uncles.

Growing up I never heard much about Grandma and Grandpa Komp. They both died before I was born. But last year Dad's customary reserve was suddenly gone, and he spoke of his father with tears in his eyes. "He was a Bible scholar," he told me. I had never heard that before. "I wish he was here," Dad said, taking my hand as I never remember him doing when I was a child. "My father was very affectionate." I never would have guessed that either!

Perhaps I can never fathom the ways his father and mother were a part of him. For certain, a part of them lives on with me. Today I give "Grandma and Grandpa" a safe high shelf in my own china cabinet. And I give them a part of my heart as well as I link my family's present with the legacy Grandma and Grandpa passed on to me.

☞ HEARTBEAT: *Recall a part of your past that reminds you that God has chosen to be known as your parent.*

_____

_____

_____

_____

_____

_____

_____

_____

_____

5
GENTLE COMPANIONS

Tell me thy company, and I'll tell thee what thou art.

Miguel de Cervantes

1

A KIND OLD WOMAN

The older women can train the younger women to be self-controlled and kind.

Titus 2:3–4 ADAPTED

I got to know Edna at a local breakfast eatery where I often found her sitting at a table writing notes to shut-ins. Edna transformed small town news, passed on by a waitress, into a ministry of caring. She was missing from her usual table one morning because she was in my hospital—as a patient.

Edna was in the radiology suite when I found her with a resident physician poised over her left foot. Blue marks on Edna's arms and feet told the history of failed attempts to place an IV. Dr. Kate looked angry and frustrated as she surveyed the dozen elderly veins that had already shown their fragility and "blown." I held my tongue for the moment on the subject of veins.

Standing at Edna's side, I held her hand and talked to my young colleague about breakfast at Basems and how I had come to love this old woman. Soon, Kate put down the needle. Her face softened as she looked up the length of the hard, cold table. She hadn't noticed Edna's remarkable blue eyes before. Instead of an illusory vein with a person attached, Kate saw a fellow human enduring a young doctor's attempts to start a difficult IV.

"I'm a pediatrician." I introduced myself to Dr. Kate. "I can get an IV into anyone. May I give it a try?" The young woman nodded gratefully, and I got it in on the first stick. Instead of watching my hands to learn my IV tricks, Kate watched Edna's eyes.

Edna got her test finished, and I think Dr. Kate got what this older woman physician was trying to teach her that day. And I was reminded that there are far better ways than lectures to pass on to younger people what they need to know.

    ✍ HEARTBEAT: *Name something precious that you learned from someone older. How can you pass that along to a younger person today?*

2

A COMPASSIONATE MONK

As he went ashore he saw a great throng; and he had compassion on them.

Matthew 14:14 RSV

It was a warm spring day with wildflowers underfoot. A friend and I were staying at a monastery in the Ozark mountains, renewing friendship with the guest master of the abbey, Father Theodore. Trappist Ted had a talent for finding vivid ways to teach a simple gospel message, and I was eager for my next lesson.

Michael and I went hiking and cut across a sunlit meadow. Somehow we missed the right trail and came out at the base of a ridge instead of on its plateau. Michael pointed to the shortest path to our destination—straight up the ridge. Halfway there, I felt the pain in my lower back that signaled a muscle spasm.

No longer able to walk, I hunched over to escape the pain. I was an odd sight in the perpendicular, but that was the only position that took away my pain. When we arrived back at the guest house for lunch, I was still bent over.

A shadow crossed in front of me in the dining room, and I found myself nose to nose with Father Ted. He was bent into the same position that I was, imitating my distress. "Di," he said with a twinkle in his eye, "could you give me a clue what the correct pastoral response is to this most unusual situation?"

"Father," I replied, amused by his empathic mimicry, "compassion does not require that you be bent like I am."

An orthopedic surgeon, who was also a guest, gave me a muscle relaxant. I enjoyed a good nap and awoke able to stand up straight.

From Father Ted this doctor learned that medication comes after understanding in order of priority. Compassion—sharing someone else's point of view—is always the correct pastoral, medical, and personal response to any situation.

☞ HEARTBEAT: *Put yourself in the place of someone who is hurting. Can you think of three ways that you could better understand them by imagining their point of view?*

3

A PRECIOUS SPARROW

Two sparrows are sold for a farthing, aren't they? Yet not a single sparrow falls to the ground without your Father's knowledge. Never be afraid, then—you are far more valuable than sparrows.

Matthew 10:29, 31 JBP

When Karen came to the house to talk, she slumped forward in a chair as if she were carrying a heavy burden on her shoulders. Her older brother was getting on with his life, but this teenager still lived at home with her parents. Mom and Dad's troubled lives seemed to weigh her down. As I listened to this sad girl, an incident came to me from the day before.

Two baby sparrows had fallen from a nest. One was strong enough to fly away, but the other would have perished if a young neighbor hadn't taken him home to nurse him back to health. The child knew that the day was coming when he must encourage "Peepser" back to his own world. For now the frail bird was content in his makeshift nest.

At that moment I had another little sparrow before me. So I shared this story with my young friend, wondering what it might say to her. Tears flooded Karen's eyes, and she sat up straight in her chair, relieved. "Thank you," she whispered. "That story really speaks to my situation."

Karen recognized herself and her brother in Peepser's story, including the hospitable "nest" she had found within her local church. She spoke fondly of a married couple who served as advisers for her youth group. In the rest and restoration she received from that church family, Karen realized that her loving heavenly Father had not forgotten her after all.

Until Karen told me about her hospitable nest, I didn't realize why Peepser's story so deeply impressed me. In my photo album I found a snapshot of Fred and Irene. This young pastor and his bride—now his widow—were kind to my sister and me when we were Karen's age. I wrote Irene a letter today, enclosing that photo and this story.

God would not let Karen fall. Nor will he forget Irene or you or me.

❧ HEARTBEAT: *Recall someone God used to make a hospitable nest for you. Write them a letter to tell them how it changed your life.*

4

A TENDER SYNAPSE

Planted in the house of Yahweh, [the right-
eous] will flourish in the courts of our God,
still bearing fruit in old age, still remaining
green and fresh.

Psalm 92:14 JB

Orchids are not only beautiful flowers to look at, they can introduce you to beautiful people. Some years ago, my sister and I called
on a retired doctor in upstate New York. As soon as we read about
him in the local newspaper, we were eager to meet this famous local
orchid fancier.

We heard an awful racket that sounded like a freight train being
derailed when we drove up to the house. "Look," Marge said excit-
edly, "he raises peacocks too!" A half-dozen or so of these comely
creatures pranced about the yard. Here was a man of imagination
who welcomed some of God's most exotic creations into his life.

As we entered the greenhouse, the scent of a vanilla bean plant
filled the air. We were surrounded by hundreds of the most handsome
flowers I had ever seen. Big *Cattleyas* and tiny *Oncidia* thrived in Dr.
Sidney's garden of love.

We were captivated by this elderly but quick-witted physician.
After an hour of contemplating Latin-labeled hybrids, we reached a
plant that gave him special pride. Sidney lovingly took it in his arms

and gently fingered the breathtaking spray of yellow blooms. He started to recite its ancestry, but the names of its parents just would not come. He thought for another moment and then shook his head.

"Whoops!" he grinned. "I just burned out another synapse." Then he laughed, and we laughed with him.

These days, I recall more than my elderly friend's beautiful orchids in all their majestic colors. I remember with fondness the gracious orchid grower who taught me a tenderness with the self. Now when my own brain slows down, I can take it in stride. Instead of berating myself, I say, "Whoops! I just burned out another synapse." These simple words cut down greatly on any self-condemnation. And they help me to flower into a more lovely human being.

❤ HEARTBEAT: *Identify an area of your life where you are tough on yourself and be gentle there today.*

5

A GREEK REVELATION

I, John ... was on the island of Patmos because of the word of God and the testimony of Jesus.

Revelation 1:9 NIV

Walking down the mountain from the cave on the Greek island of Patmos where John received his mysterious Revelation, I could see the sparkling Aegean Sea.

I strolled down a side street to avoid the hot afternoon sun and came across a toothless old woman sweeping the street. She (who spoke no English) greeted me (who spoke no Greek), and I returned her greeting with a smile. She motioned for me to join her on her shaded balcony, and I acquiesced.

To her amazement, I drank the thick Greek coffee she offered me without sweetener. She chattered away in Greek patois, gesturing expressively and fingering her wedding band. I sensed her continuing grief over the loss of her husband. "Was I married?" she wondered, taking my hands, searching in vain for a golden band. I gathered that her children did not visit often enough. "What do you think of the holy cave?" she asked, waving in the direction of *Apocalypse*. "A place to find *Christus*," I replied, and she nodded that she knew exactly what I meant.

For an hour we sipped and chatted, unimpeded by words, sharing thoughts and emotions by the glance of an eye, the movements of the hand. By our presence. Then she shuffled off in torn house slippers to water the beloved plants that shaded her balcony, reciting each of their histories. When we parted, she made a bouquet for me of fragrant small white blossoms fit for a bride, and she kissed me on both cheeks.

What a wonderful gift, making this new friend. I had always imagined John on a deserted isle with a secretary and two goats. Perhaps it was because he strolled down streets just like this one that he was able to receive that great vision of Jesus. I try to slow down in my very busy life today, remembering this chance encounter on a Greek isle, waiting to meet other people God has prepared for my day.

☞ HEARTBEAT: *Look for a side street that God has in store for you today and identify someone special who waits to meet you there.*

_____

_____

_____

_____

_____

_____

_____

_____

_____

_____

_____

6

BETWEEN A ROCK AND A HARD PLACE

The art of living is more like wrestling than dancing.
Marcus Aurelius Antonius

1

BETWEEN A ROCK
AND A HARD PLACE

*The LORD is my rock, my fortress and my
deliverer; my God is my rock, in whom I take
refuge.*

Psalm 18:2 NIV

To get to Yale I drive across the Quinnipiac Bridge that links
the shoreline towns of eastern Connecticut with New Haven. In the
language of the Native Americans who named the river that the
bridge spans, Quinnipiac means "between two rocks." I see these
landmarks towering over the landscape every morning, "East Rock"
and "West Rock."

Soon after I started work at Yale, I read in the New Haven Reg-
ister that so many people have a phobia for the "Q" Bridge that a
psychiatrist in New Haven specializes in the treatment of its suffer-
ers! For his patients, Quinnipiac translates as "between a rock and
a hard place."

Now, I know something about bridge phobia myself. My heart
races when I approach a narrow, high-arching span. My knuckles
blanch when I see a steel grid deck. But after a few months of smooth
sailing over the wide, low, and well-paved Quinnipiac Bridge, I real-

ized that Q-phobia had little to do with the structure of the bridge itself and a lot to do with fear of a job.

Unlike those who took to that psychiatrist's couch, I loved my new job with a passion. I knew what lay on each side of the bridge. To the east is my woodland refuge where I can escape after a strenuous day. To the west is the medical school where I take care of children with cancer and contribute to the education of young doctors. In both places I have seen evidence of God.

The double rocks provide a most fitting metaphor to describe my very complicated life. Sometimes my life's journey is fearful, but whichever direction I'm traveling, God is there! God is my Rock—and the Lord of my hard places.

> ❦ HEARTBEAT: *Recall a time in your life when you were caught between two fears. Describe how Christ guided you between and through them.*

2

WEASEL WORDSMITH

His speech is smooth as butter, yet war is in his heart; his words are more soothing than oil, yet they are drawn swords.

Psalm 55:21 NIV

An English colleague was so alarmed by the cutbacks in Great Britain's National Health Service that he wrote a carefully worded letter to his hospital administrator to express his concerns. Weeks passed without an answer, so he stopped by to ask the administrator why he had not replied. "Ah, yes," came the answer. "I was waiting until I found the right 'weasel words' to use."

Ah, weasel words! I know the concept well. Smooth and seemingly soothing at the time they are spoken, these words do not bring healing to a situation. Weasel words hurt because they come from someone whom we believe to be on our side. "If an enemy were insulting me, I could endure it.... But it is you, a man like myself, my companion, my close friend" (Psalm 55:12–13 NIV).

My colleague's dilemma brought weasel words of my own to mind. I recall talking to the parents of a sick child who pleaded with me to tell them everything. I knew the grim news, but I suggested that we wait until "all the results were in" to talk. Like that hospital administrator, I wanted to procrastinate until I could find a more palatable way to phrase the news. But that time never came. The relationship broke down, and all confidence was lost.

I keep a daily note in my journal now of my weasel words. This week I charted two: "I know that went out in the mail yesterday," and "Can I get back to you later today?" I hope that as I pray over these phrases, they will slink out of my vocabulary and simply disappear.

> ✒ HEARTBEAT: *Record an example of your own "weasel words." Translate them into words that are pleasing in the sight of the Lord.*

_____

_____

_____

_____

_____

_____

_____

_____

_____

_____

_____

_____

_____

3

THE CASE OF TABLED TEARS

Then turning toward the woman, [Jesus] said to Simon, "Do you see this woman? I entered your house; you gave me no water for my feet, but she has bathed my feet with her tears and dried them with her hair."

Luke 7:44 NRSV

We crossed the street to the hospital together, a young doctor and I, to see a new patient, and to speak with his young parents. Our double reflections were mirrored in a window as we walked across the bridge to the Children's Hospital. Barb is bright and thorough. (So was I at her age.) But I, her teacher, had something she did not possess—decades of experience in our specialty.

When we reached the ward, the mother of this desperately ill baby spoke to us tearfully and bluntly. She didn't back off from asking the toughest questions and kept her tear-stained eyes focused on Barb's. Something told me to stay in the wings this time, bow off the center stage. I stood behind the parents and let my younger colleague speak.

When we left the room together an hour later, I saw tears fill Barbara's eyes. I didn't catch the tears in her voice in the room as she spoke. I heard only a careful, compassionate explanation. What if this young doctor had broken down while we were with the family? The parents might have concluded that their child was totally without hope. No, her tears waited for the proper time, when her task was complete.

Barb brought credentials of her own to that encounter that I cannot claim. She has a baby the same age as our little patient. And a husband with cancer who just went through heavy treatment himself. She didn't say this to the parents in so many words. But the tone of Barb's voice and the gentleness of her eyes communicated something rare. *Yes! I really do understand!*

Early in medical school I was careful to put away my tears. I'm sure Jesus' host, Simon the Pharisee, had been careful to do the same. Big boys and big doctors don't cry. Like me, Simon was proud of his position. But Jesus taught him—and me—a different lesson. I went into that room proud of my gray hair and professional experience. I left humbled by a young woman's tears.

✿ HEARTBEAT: *Keep track today of situations in which you feel highly self-confident. Watch for God to take something that makes you feel uncomfortable and use it to teach you about your relationship with him and others.*

4

IT IS ENOUGH

[Elijah] went a day's journey into the wilderness, and came and sat down under a juniper tree: and he requested for himself that he might die; and said, It is enough; now, O LORD, take away my life.

1 Kings 19:4 KJV

Through taped auditions, our community Oratorio Society located what we believed to be a baritone winner for our annual concert of great sacred music, this year, Mendelssohn's *Elijah*. Or so we thought.

The weekend of our major concert, I was the one responsible for our guest soloist. I met "Elijah" at our airport Saturday afternoon and whisked him off to the tuxedo shop. From there we went on to the dress rehearsal. Our chorus had practiced for months, and we were waiting with excitement to hear our soloist in person. But when our hero tried to reproduce what we had heard on tape without the benefit of a microphone, his voice simply was not strong enough.

Later that evening, "Elijah" disappeared after the rehearsal. I could not find him. My phone rang all night. And the next morning. Finally, only hours before the concert, the director went over to Elijah's guest quarters and found our baritone holed up in humiliation. Like the angel that ministered to the first Elijah in the desert, the director assured the depressed young man of our desire to work with the gifts that he had, rather than harshly judge him for any deficiencies.

That evening, Elijah's performance was enough. He did his best. More importantly, a young singer learned that some people were actually listening to the words he sang. And I, a perfectionist, am now on the lookout for angels when I think I've failed and judge myself too harshly.

☞ HEARTBEAT: *Identify an area of your life where you judge yourself harshly. Describe a time that you thought you failed but your actions were more than enough to please God.*

_____

_____

_____

_____

_____

_____

_____

_____

_____

_____

_____

_____

5

THE RECURRENT CROSS

For the message about the cross is foolishness to those who are perishing, but to us who are being saved it is the power of God.

1 Corinthians 1:18 NRSV

John rushed to the hospital as soon as he heard about the motorcycle accident. His brother's injuries were so severe that they thought he might not live through the night. As he looked out the waiting room window, John saw a lonely illuminated cross shining on a nearby mountain. He began to pray.

"If my brother lives," John told God, "I will lead a good life. I'll even give up smoking!" He thought about other bargaining chips that he might have with God. But his brother died. John looked at the cross one more time with anger and felt his faith perish.

John married, raised a family, discontinued any contact with the church—and continued to smoke. That was many years ago. Then he found himself back in the same hospital waiting room. This time his son lay close to death.

Matt writhed in pain, clutching his belly. The child was too tired to cry. There was an ominous yellow cast to his skin. Cancer! At that moment John looked out the same window and saw that same cross, still shining on the same mountain.

He could hardly believe that this was happening to him a second time. This time John had no bargaining chips. He made no offers. He simply, humbly put his life in the hands of the One who had hung on a cross. John surrendered his life and his family to God.

Matt has more than survived. He completed his treatment a few years back and has no evidence of cancer today.* At ten years of age, he prays for other children with cancer! And Matt's dad? John learned that the power of God belongs to those who know that they have nothing to offer Jesus except their hearts.

I watch John gather his family into his arms today and think about all the times I've told God what I would do for him. But all he has ever wanted from me is to acknowledge my own powerlessness and look to the Cross for my aid. What a foolish person I have been!

☙ HEARTBEAT: *Remember a time when the cross of Christ seemed like foolishness to you. Now think of a time when you understood the same cross to be power from God for your life.*

---

*Matt's story is told in "A Child Shall Lead Them" in *Images of Grace: A Pediatrician's Trilogy of Faith, Hope, and Love* (Grand Rapids: Zondervan, 1996).

7

CINNAMON BUNS
IN CYBERSPACE

*The Holy Supper is kept not [in]
what we give but what we share.*
James Russell Lowell

1

TASTING THE BREAD OF LIFE

O taste and see that the LORD is good.
Psalm 34:8 KJV

The Rev. Ken Norris excused himself shortly before the organ began to play. "I need to turn on the oven to warm up the bread," he explained. This was to be a special Ash Wednesday service to remember a year with many famines in the world. Soon the deacons entered and placed the elements on the Communion table. The fragrant aroma of hot bread filled the sanctuary.

"Almighty God," we prayed, "you whose own Son had to flee the evil plans of King Herod and seek refuge in a strange land, we bring before you the needs of the many refugees throughout the world, particularly those in Africa." After this shared prayer written by African Christians, we gathered at the altar to eat and drink in the name of Jesus Christ. There were three Communion breads, each based on a recipe from a different African country. Sourdough *ksra* from Morocco. Cardamom-seasoned *mahamri* from Kenya. And small fried cakes of *diphaphata* from Botswana.

The warm, fragrant breads tasted so good that instead of taking one small piece the way we usually did, we just had to sample from each of the loaves. We could not look down or close our eyes after our first taste. We had to have eye contact with someone else at the altar to share the mystery. How good it tasted! We lingered there rather than return to isolating pews.

I looked around at the others in the circle that was gathered. No one wanted to leave this love-feast meal. This is how the Holy Supper was meant to be kept. When I taste how good the Lord is, my first reaction is to share the good news with someone else. "My word, did you taste how delicious that Bread was? I just can't go home yet!"

❧ HEARTBEAT: *Think of a way in which you have tasted God's goodness this week. Name someone with whom you will share that good news.*

_____

_____

_____

_____

_____

_____

_____

_____

_____

_____

_____

2

CINNAMON BUNS
IN CYBERSPACE

*Therefore confess your sins to each other and
pray for each other so that you may be healed.*
James 5:16 NIV

Saturday morning Joyce kissed her sleeping husband and
slipped out of bed. She plugged in Mr. Coffee and sat down at the computer she uses during the week to do the billing for her husband's firm.
After a few simple keyboard commands, "ReJoyce" entered a cyberspace chat room known as "Fellowship Hall."*

"@@@@@@@" she typed in. "Anyone like a cinnamon bun?"
Joyce asked, hoping to find someone else who was up at 6 a.m. Chicago time.

"Mmmmmm," raved ImaMom from Memphis in return. "Do they
ever smell yummy!"

"Catcha cupa mocha java! :::::::: c|_| ::::::" offered RN4JC, too tired
to sleep after the late shift in a Honolulu emergency room.

Carrying a heavy burden she wanted to put down, "ReJoyce"
entered Fellowship Hall as if it were a confessional. A friend had confided a similar problem to their pastor's wife last year, and now everyone in the church seemed to know. Joyce chose instead to talk to

someone she had never met in person who could respect her need for confidentiality—"Doktor Di."

I could sense her tears as ReJoyce typed in her confession for me to see. She spoke of a flirtation with a man in her church choir that had grown into an obsession for affection. ReJoyce put down her heavy weight with her words. As she confessed her sin to God in my presence, she spoke of her intention not to repeat it.

"{{{{{{Doktor Di}}}}}}" appeared on my computer screen when she finished her prayer. The brackets surrounding my screen name were a holy cyberhug, ReJoyce's benediction to her own prayer.

As a wounded person, Joyce found the people in her church too intimidating to entrust with her secret. She needed me to listen and repeat God's words of pardon. Her confidence in me that day reminded me that sometimes "Doktor Di" can be quite overwhelming in person. It takes practice to learn how to love someone back into the arms of God.

Who would ever have thought of the information superhighway as a place where God could teach a doctor how to listen. I want the Great Physician to teach "Doktor Di" more about these things that I never learned in medical school.

☞ HEARTBEAT: *Look for someone today who needs healing through a gentle Christian presence.*

_____

*"Fellowship Hall" is a computer network chat room in Christianity Online's segment of America Online where people can carry on conversations with each other.

3

NO MORE DARKNESS

Sing to the LORD a new song, his praise in the assembly of the saints.

Psalm 149:1 NIV

There is a teenager named "DarkNESS" who flamed into Fellowship Hall some mornings to disrupt our pious chat. People reacted to this young hellion in different ways. My first response was to line out the words of the hymn "A Mighty Fortress Is Our God." I was very proud of myself as I typed, "The prince of DarkNESS grim, we tremble not for him . . . for lo, his doom is sure." That drove DarkNESS berserk. He fled Fellowship Hall at the sound of my "voice."

The next morning I found Pop 41, the father of a teenage girl with cancer, already there in Fellowship Hall when I logged on. Marcy was in the hospital that week for heavy-duty chemo. As I watched the chat on my computer screen, I saw Pop 41 talking to someone named "Carl," but no one by that name was listed in the chat room. But there was DarkNESS. Pop 41 signaled me privately. "Don't call him DarkNESS. He's a hurting kid. Call him by his real name instead."

I watched a miracle unfold as the Father-heart of God reached across all of cyberspace to minister to a wounded boy through a suffering human dad. Carl began to behave like a friendly member of our breakfast fellowship.

I woke up early a few days later. DarkNESS was already there in Fellowship Hall. I "sang" a different song, one that woke my soul early that morning: "I will change your name. You shall no longer be called: wounded, outcast, lonely, or afraid . . . I will change your name. Your new name shall be: confidence, joyfulness, overcoming one, faithfulness, friend of God, one who sees my face."*

"Who are you singing that for?" DarkNESS asked.

"For you," I told him.

DarkNESS didn't answer me with words. If you look sideways, you'll understand what he typed :-). It's a smiley face. I hugged him in response—{{{{{{{Carl}}}}}}}—and then signed off.

A boy who called himself DarkNESS taught me to change my tune so I could reach into the darkness to embrace a wounded kid.

☞ HEARTBEAT: *Browse through a hymn book or collection of praise songs. Find a song new to you that speaks of some area where God is trying to change your life.*

_____

_____

_____

_____

_____

_____

_____

*By D. J. Butler, copyright Mercy Publishers.

4

PREACHER PUP
AND THE PEW POTATOES

*Be shepherds of God's flock that is under your
care . . . as God wants you to be . . . eager to serve.*
1 Peter 5:2 NIV

Both sheep and shepherds seem to be in trouble these days, and both are coming by the droves to Christian cyberspace. In Fellowship Hall, pastors tell me about the poor preparation they received in seminary for the realities of congregational life. Some of their churches are filled with the unrealistic expectations of pew potatoes who seem to do nothing but sit there on Sundays like starchy lumps.

It was in this strange electronic world that I met a teenager who feels called into ordained ministry. I'm honored to call this preacher pup my friend. Brad writes long letters to "Doktor Di" about his home church. This young man knows that a pastor's job is more than writing a sermon once a week. His exciting narratives about Pastor Bob's ministry read like blow-by-blow reports written from a ringside seat at a major sporting event.

There was a tragedy a few months back—the untimely death of a young friend. Pastor Bob took Brad with him on his rounds: visiting the family, calling at the funeral home. Brad was there for all the painful parts. Bob censored nothing. When it was over, he sat the boy down. He told him about the important work of a "gutter pastor"—a shepherd who goes where the sheep are.

Last week I lost my dad. Some of my friends offered me pop psychology rather than solace. I didn't want to talk about my feelings; I just wanted to talk about my dad. But along came a preacher pup who sat down beside me in my cybergutter. He didn't ask me about my feelings—he told me about his own. Brad signed his e-mail "from a kid who really loves you."

Nope, no pew potatoes vegetating in that church. And preacher pups can test their callings as they observe a proper shepherd of the sheep. This little cyberlamb is surely grateful.

❦ HEARTBEAT: *On Sunday, note a part of your pastor's job description that you never paid attention to before. Discover how that part of your pastor's work helps you carry out your own "calling."*

5

THE ONE WHO SHARES BREAD

Cast your bread upon the waters, for after many days you will find it again.

Ecclesiastes 11:1 NIV

Our family name is so rare that I wondered where we came from. Eventually, I set out to dig up the family roots. In the process, I learned a lot about our name—and myself as well. Growing up, I used to check the New York City telephone directory to see if there was anyone else named "Komp." As a grownup, I spent one rainy Saturday in Yale's Sterling Memorial Library copying down every Komp name and address out of every telephone directory in their vast collection.

The Komps came from a farm in the Vogelsberg area of Hessen that has some of the poorest sod in Germany. Sometimes the landed aristocracy taxed poor farmers like my ancestors so heavily that they were left without bread to eat. When they set out on a three-month sea voyage to the New World in the early 1800s, the ship ran out of bread en route, and they had only sauerkraut to eat for the final week!

Although the Komps came from Germany, I learned that our name isn't really German in origin. The family left France in a time of religious persecution. In Germany they shortened the name from Kompenhans to Komp. And what did Kompenhans mean? The Latin roots are the same as the word "companion"—*cum panis*. The one who shares bread.

When I visited the tiny farm villages of the Vogelsberg, it was strange to see my family name inscribed on so many headstones. But all of this genealogical research has given me something pleasant to consider when I prepare a meal for friends. Now I think of my name as a "calling." My name has become something to try to live up to by sharing what I can.

🖤 HEARTBEAT: *Learn the meaning of either your first or last name. Determine what in your name is worth living up to.*

8
HOME AWAY FROM HOME

In literature the longing for home is found in the stories of paradise, of the forgotten places where we once belonged.

Madeleine L'Engle

1

HOME AWAY FROM HOME

"If you consider me a believer in the Lord,"
she said, "come and stay at my house." And
she persuaded us.

Acts 16:15 NIV

Have you ever arrived in a strange city and had the sense that you just came home? That was how an ordinary tourist adventure with one of my German cousins turned out. Reluctantly, Hasso left me in the medieval university town of Marburg by myself. "You won't meet anyone," he warned me. "You still don't understand how reserved Germans are."

Marburg was a page out of a Grimm brothers' tale. Situated on top of a hill, it was encircled by perfectly preserved half-timber houses and lined with cobblestone streets. The marketplace bustled with vegetable and flower vendors. It wasn't until I backed up in the Marktplatz to get a wide-angle photo of the magnificent *Rathaus* that I saw a Christian bookstore.

The manager, Elke, greeted me when I entered. While I was browsing through books, her husband, Roland, brought me coffee. They invited me to go home with them for the evening.

The bookstore was a small beginning of what is now a large Christian ministry. A small band of university students tithed their nonexistent salaries to open the shop. There was a worship service in a chapel in the cellar in those days called "Christus-Treff"—an encounter with Christ. About forty college-aged kids came every Thursday night in those early days. Twelve years later, the bookstore is still going strong, but Christus-Treff has moved into a church large enough to accommodate the three hundred or more people from different Christian traditions who want to worship together and build each other up in the faith.

Over the years I've become part of that ministry as well. Two sabbatical years in Marburg have secured my place as a "Christus-Treffler." I enjoy my assignments with German medical students and English-speaking refugees. (I keep them up today on my business trips back.)

What started as a simple act of hospitality for a stranger became a building block for the kingdom of heaven. No wonder I was persuaded to make Marburg my home away from home.

☞ HEARTBEAT: *Is there a place other than your hometown where you feel at home? Give three reasons why it reminds you of heaven.*

2

A MIGHTY FORTRESS

The LORD is my rock, my fortress, and my deliverer, my God, my rock in whom I take refuge.
Psalm 18:2 NRSV

"Marburg! Here Marburg!" A fortified castle crowns her landscape. When I see that proud facade on the hill in the distance, I know that the train conductor will soon shout out that I am coming home. Twelve years after my first visit, that view still excites me when the train rounds the bend.

Marburg! Here is Marburg: eleven clean-cut, casually dressed young adults posing for a snapshot at the same castle. The photo sits on my desk in Connecticut. Six of the eleven Christus-Trefflers pictured there are young doctors. One of them I've known since the first day he started pre-med. Matthias and I have gone for walks in the castle garden together, talking long hours about what it means to be a Christian doctor.

I treasure these moments one-on-one with Germany's future doctors. The memory of a widow I met on a train to Frankfurt after one of these chats remains in my heart. She lamented her family doctor's attitude when her husband died of cancer. "How can you help someone die if you don't believe God?" she asked him. The doctor looked away. The widow was encouraged to hear about my student friends.

Martin Luther visited Marburg. Perhaps my mighty fortress was his own. This bulwark has failed a time or two over the centuries, and sandblasters are busily at work this year. Whenever I'm in Marburg, I take my laptop computer up to the castle garden to work. I look down over the wall at the city below and feel like a co-owner of the whole wide world.

The photo of my friends and the castle reminds me that God is a mighty fortress—and much more. Unlike the castle, God doesn't just stand there and look awesome. He's the head of a royal family of which Matthias and I and these other dear friends are a part.

☞ HEARTBEAT: *Recall an incident in your life that reminded you that your Father is a King.*

_____

_____

_____

_____

_____

_____

_____

_____

_____

---

*The full story is told in "Journey to Disbelief" in *A Window to Heaven: When Children See Life in Death* (Grand Rapids: Zondervan, 1992).

3

A SERVANT'S FORM

Let the same mind be in you that was in Christ Jesus, who . . . did not regard equality with God as something to be exploited, but emptied himself, taking the form of a slave.

Philippians 2:5–7 NRSV

From the castle, you can look down onto the city below and see Marburg's other famous edifice, St. Elisabeth's Church. This year Elisabeth is wearing a green beehive on one of her church towers—scaffolding for the stonemasons. The church is about the same age as the castle. She also badly needs a face-lift.

Built in the same century, the castle and the church seem so far apart. Spiritually, they come from two different worlds. But this is the way Elisabeth, Queen of Thüringen, intended it to be.

Although she was of royal descent, Elisabeth didn't choose to build herself a castle when she moved to Marburg in 1228. The queen lived a simple lifestyle with the people in the town below. Her royal relations in Thüringen seemed glad to rid themselves of this pesky young widow who took Christianity far too seriously for their taste.

Rather than enjoy her wealth and privilege, Elisabeth chose to nurse the poor and dying. She died among the poor three years later, at the age of twenty-four. When a church was built to remember her ministry, it was placed where she had been—down below, among the common people.

Elisabeth reminds me what it truly means to be a child of the King. Although she had the privilege to stroll in gardens like the ones I love, looking down at the world below, she chose like Jesus to descend. The sovereign became a servant.

I love to sit in the castle garden above the city and write, the way I did today. It was peaceful and serene, but I could only stay for a while. An old man was struggling to walk back down from the castle to the retirement home at the base of the hill. I closed my laptop and gave him my arm, for his faltering step reminded me that a child of the King is a servant as well as an heir.

☞ HEARTBEAT: *Name someone whose life illustrated Jesus' style of servant leadership in a way that you could understand.*

_____

_____

_____

_____

_____

_____

_____

_____

_____

4

A LITTLE FOR JESUS

*Here is a boy with five small barley loaves and
two small fish, but how far will they go among
so many?*

John 6:9 NIV

*Freundschaftsbezeigungenstadtverordnetenversammlungen-
familieneigenthümlichkeiten.* What Mark Twain called "that awful
German language" remained an obstacle to my enjoyment of Germany. I dropped German after one miserable semester in college. The
professor seemed relieved by my departure.

At the age of forty-five I felt impelled to try again, so I entered
language school in the northern German city of Bremen and found
myself the oldest student in the class. "Grundstufe-Zwei" at Goethe
Institut was presided over by a teacher who promptly corrected any
error. It was Herr Austin's classroom all over again. For fear of cor-
rection, I spoke less German after two weeks than I had upon arrival.

I found a wonderful church in Bremen, but it too seemed a burden of words. Each Sunday I felt weighed down by my deficiencies.
Most weeks I wondered if I would even understand what the preacher had to say. A sermon could be a half hour or more of German to
muddle through!

One Sunday, Pastor Bierbaum preached about the feeding of the
five thousand. I managed to understand the Scripture text as well as

one other sentence that he repeated again and again: "Take the little you have and give it to Jesus."

That simple message was a tremendous help with my dilemma. It still is: "Take the little German you have and give it to Jesus." In retrospect, I think God planned this all to help me concentrate on the few words in that sermon that I needed to hear.

My German is still far from perfect, and I sometimes wonder whether I should even bother trying to speak it. But in my heart I see Jesus standing before me saying, "Child, do you have anything to eat?" I take my little loaf of German and give it to him. I've seen my words sink into hearts and translate crippling fears into healing tears. Even my "crumbs" can be more than enough.

☙ HEARTBEAT: *Think of something in your life you consider to be a crumb that you can give to Jesus for him to multiply and use.*

_____

_____

_____

_____

_____

_____

_____

---

*Twain invents this mythical (but entirely possible) German word in "A Tramp Abroad."

5

THE SPIRIT'S PULPIT

*Whoever speaks must do so as one speaking
the very words of God . . . Likewise the Spirit
helps us in our weakness.*

1 Peter 4:11; Romans 8:26 NRSV

My "crumbs of German" were put to a major test when I was invited to lecture at the University of Ulm in southern Germany. I didn't know what I was going to say to the students that night. How could I bring a message of hope to a secular modern university? How could my little German ever be enough?

One of the students took me on a tour of the city. As he pointed out each magnificent piece of artwork in the cathedral, my mind raced between the exquisite Gothic woodwork and the task that lay before me that evening. Finally, we came to the stately pulpit with its intricately carved sounding board.

Microphones had not yet been invented when this magnificent church was designed. Architects of the time did their best with what they knew about acoustics to make sure that the people could hear the sermon. So they designed a wooden sounding board, placed above the preacher's head, that effectively transmitted sound throughout the cavernous open space of the cathedral.

Carved into this sounding board is a reproduction of the pulpit itself, including the intricately carved steps leading up to where the preacher stands. This "pulpit above the pulpit" is a symbolic reminder to both pastor and congregation that human words do not suffice in declaring the Good News. A higher Preacher, the Holy Spirit, must be allowed to speak whenever the Word is proclaimed.

This handsome piece of ancient church furniture was just the reminder that I needed about my lecture that evening. My words would not matter at all. If I had anything to say worth hearing, the Spirit of God would give me the words.

☞ HEARTBEAT: *Find a situation today where you have an opportunity to share the Good News. Record how God's Spirit gives shape to your words.*

9
TABLE TALK

Let us join ('tis God commands). Let us join our hearts and hands, help to gain our calling's hope, build we each the other up. God his blessing shall dispense, God shall crown his ordinance, meet in his appointed ways, nourish us with social grace.

Charles Wesley

1

FIVE WERE INVITED,
BUT TEN APPEARED

*So then, my brothers and sisters, when you
come together to eat, wait for one another.*
1 Corinthians 11:33 NRSV

Near the entrance to an apartment in a quaint half-timbered
house directly beneath Marburg's castle is a sign that Roland and Elke
have hung for our reminder: "Blessed Are The Flexible, For They Shall
Not Break." During my last sabbatical year in Germany, I was one of
eight Christus-Trefflers who lived in that house.

On days that I was writing, I worked at home and cooked our
shared midday meals. This was always a challenge, since we never
knew how many people would be at the table. I was expecting five one
day, but the group had mysteriously expanded to eight before the table
was even set. More vegetables and chicken were plopped into the pot.
By the time we said grace, we numbered ten because Roland came
home with two stray friends who just "happened to be in the neighborhood" at mealtime.

This was quite unlike some of my famous feasts in America over
the years. I remember making dainty little Cornish hens for one dinner
party, each bird dressed with a different stuffing. There was no room for
unexpected guests at that feast. Another time I offered a crown roast

of lamb for the main course. One pantied chop too few would have made a meager meal. No, I must admit that there hasn't been much room for the unexpected in my life.

Standing over the stove in Marburg, I tossed a few more carrots into the pot, knowing exactly how I would apply this lesson when my sabbatical was ancient history. My students at Yale don't know the meaning of the phrase "RSVP." But there's a more important phrase that I've had to learn, taken from a German proverb: "Five were invited, ten appeared. Throw water in the soup and tell them all they're welcome." I cross-stitched this adage onto a linen kitchen towel, now hanging on my refrigerator door in Connecticut. You'll also find an immense pot on the stove—in case you ever drop in on me unexpectedly.

HEARTBEAT: Identify an area of your life where you need to be more flexible.

2

A REFINER'S FIRE

The promises of the LORD are promises that are pure, silver refined in a furnace on the ground, purified seven times.

Psalm 12:6 NRSV

Ramazi is a friend who came from the Republic of Georgia to visit Christus-Treff. His first personal encounter with Christ came shortly after the fall of the Soviet empire. Now that he was in Germany, he wondered what it would mean to grow as a Christian when he returned to Georgia.

To be certain that we would remember his visit, Ramazi made a brass plaque for our Steinweg-Haus. He had hammered the words into the stiff metal. Had he been at home in Georgia in his own metal shop, he would have finished it differently.

"I'd place it into the fire," he said, "and let it get very, very hot. That removes the—how do you say it?—dross. When it cools," he continued, illustrating the process with his hands, "I would put it back in the fire again, time after time, until all the impurities come out of the molten metal."

I thought about that image of the refiner's fire and of the words of this young man who had grown up under an official policy of atheism. "Ramazi, that's exactly what the Bible says God does with us," I said. "God places us in the refiner's fire to remove our impurities."

The flames felt very hot to me at that moment because God was working on an area of my life that needed great refining.

Living in this house, living in a community, was a new experience for me. In Connecticut I enjoy the privacy of living alone, where I can concentrate on my work. But what will it be like when I'm elderly and dependent on other people? Perhaps living in this house is a "dry run" for future nursing home days when I won't have the option to bail out! There certainly were days in Marburg when I wished that I could.

Ramazi's eyes brightened as he thought about his workshop at home. To me, the refiner's fire is an exotic biblical metaphor, but to him it is a homey, familiar image. When he returned home, he would have all the tools he needed to understand what God wanted to do in his life. When my sabbatical was over and I headed home, I would take Ramazi's story with me to remind me what God wants to do for me as well.

☞ HEARTBEAT: *Name some "base elements" in your life. During the week, record the ways God uses to purify that part of your life.*

3

A GEORGIAN GRACE

Those who go out weeping, bearing the seed for sowing, shall come home with shouts of joy, carrying their sheaves.

Psalm 126:6 NRSV

One midday in Marburg I asked three of our table-family to bless the food we ate. I invited Johannes to pray in German, Bob to pray in English, and Ramazi to pray in Georgian. "But no one will understand me," Ramazi protested.

"Don't worry about that," I said. "God will help us understand."

The German and English prayers were brief, as the smell of a perfectly herbed stew filled the dining room. Then Ramazi began to pray in Georgian, a long, impassioned prayer. Although the exact meaning of the foreign words escaped us, the deeper sense of the prayer blessed us all. Later in the meal, Ramazi said to me, "That's the first time in my life I've ever prayed out loud. In any language." His confession made me feel doubly blessed remembering how hard it had been for me to muster up my prayer of holy *chutzpah*.

Several days later Ramazi said, "It's time for me to go home. I cannot stay away from my family and friends for very long." As a farewell gift, he gave me a cookbook of Georgian recipes printed in English.

Ramazi's life ahead in Georgia would not be easy. Just that week there had been the threat of civil war. He had come to Germany to learn more about the Christian way of life. This prayer in the language of his people reminded him that he came to Marburg for a purpose. Now he was ready to go home, carrying his harvest to his people.

There are many times I pack my own bags, anticipating a new adventure. Always, afterward, God leads me home again to share my excitement. I pray that, like Ramazi, I carry my harvest home with "grace."

🍂 HEARTBEAT: *Think about a prayer that changed your relationship with God. Why did things change?*

_____

_____

_____

_____

_____

_____

_____

_____

_____

_____

_____

_____

_____

_____

4

MARTHA'S DISTRACTION

But Martha was very worried about her elab-
orate preparations . . . "Lord, don't you mind
that my sister has left me to do everything by
myself? Tell her to come and help me."

Luke 10:40 JBP

With the help of Ramazi's cookbook, I engineered a multicourse Georgian farewell feast in his honor. It took two days to prepare the meal. My housemates would all help. Or so I thought.

An hour before we were to eat, Barbara left for the bookstore and didn't get back in time to make the salad. Roland called up the stairwell to say that he was short on time and had errands to run. No one else at home asked if I needed help until just before we sat down to eat. By that time, I had run up and down the narrow, winding stairs three times and had taken care of everything myself. After my final trek to get the rest of the food, I found Horst clearing the table I had set and replacing it with a different tablecloth and dishes. At that point, I could have killed them all.

I was not in a good mood, for I was having a Martha-day. Here are typical symptoms of her distress:

1. Martha doesn't give assignments, she waits for people to volunteer.
2. When no one volunteers, Martha gets annoyed.

3. When people do volunteer, Martha says that she doesn't need help.

After dinner, I spent some Mary-time at Jesus' feet to unload all the tension that "Martha" unnecessarily brought upon herself. If you feel the first symptoms of the Martha-disease coming on, get yourself to the Great Physician!

HEARTBEAT: *Find an area of your life where Jesus wants you to give up control. List three "symptoms" that will help you spot this problem early when it comes around again to catch you off guard.*

5

THE BEST (GERMAN) CHRISTMAS PAGEANT EVER

And at this sound, the crowd gathered and was bewildered, because each one heard them speaking in their native language.

Acts 2:6 RSV

There were many international guests at Marburg's university who would be alone at Christmastime. A veterinarian from Ethiopia told me that he had no personal contact with Germans other than shopkeepers and the friends he met from Christus-Treff. A Chinese gynecologist and a Korean psychologist had similar stories. We planned a holiday dinner and promised more than food.

Part of the entertainment that evening was an after-dinner skit. Three Chinese scholars played the "three professors from the East." Even the ersatz camels in the skit were all international students. The highlight, however, came with Roland's presentation at the end.

Roland carried a heavy sports bag onto the stage. "Anyone here whose native tongue is Korean? Arabic?" As guests raised their hands, Roland invited them to join him. He pulled a book out of the bag in their language and showed them a place to read from when their turn came. When he called out English, he beckoned for me to come up. Then he handed me a Bible, open to the same verse as all the others.

When we twenty-odd native speakers were assembled, Roland asked us to read the verse in our own language. "For God so loved the world that he gave his only begotten Son that whosoever believeth in him should not perish but have everlasting life" (John 3:16). Fired by a spark of benign nationalism, each passionate reading received a thunderous round of applause.

By the time it was my turn for English, I felt so inspired that I closed the Bible and, as one of my German friends later said, offered the King James translation "by heart and from the heart." As I left the stage, the three wise men bowed to me ceremoniously and said in broken German, "That was amazing! You look at that for thirty seconds; you got it cold!"

I certainly want that to be the only way I ever quote Scripture again. That was the way it was on Pentecost: the Good News was shared by the heart and from the heart.

☞ HEARTBEAT: *Write out a Bible verse you plan to learn by heart and to use from the depths of your heart.*

_____

_____

_____

_____

_____

_____

_____

_____

10
A GERMAN ATTIC

The resurrection is God's way of revealing to us that nothing that belongs to God will ever go to waste. Whatever belongs to God will never get lost.

Henri Nouwen

1

A SONRISE SERVICE

[Paul said:] For I think that God has exhibited us apostles as last of all.

1 Corinthians 4:9 RSV

I go back to Bremen now whenever I can to revisit the Epiphanius-Gemeinde, the church where my "little German" was given over to Jesus. The last time I worshiped there was an Easter Sunday morning.

It was dark outside when the sunrise service began. The only light in the sanctuary that morning came from the candles we all held. "Christ is the light of the world," Pastor Bierbaum proclaimed. "Christ is risen!"

We replied, "He is risen indeed!"

Dawn broke over the city as the service reached its climax. Early morning light played with the stained-glass window above the altar. I knew this window well, having seen it lit by midmorning sun. But this time a sunrise drama was unfolding. First, the white pieces of glass were illuminated. It was Jesus I saw—first faintly, then brightly. To his left, a dove appeared, as if out of nowhere. Then the yellow panes of glass caught the rising sun. A bolt of lightning appeared to the right of Jesus. As the Resurrection dawn unfolded, the rest of the picture started to fill in. Next, light aqua pieces sparkled, and I saw the waves, then the ship. Finally, I saw the disciples in the ship, afraid for their lives. The portrait was complete.

What a marvelous reflection of Easter priority this sunrise drama presented. How often I had sat in that church obsessed with myself! It takes me a long while to notice what surrounds me when I start with myself. And an even longer time before I take note of God.

Easter reverses everything. First I see the risen Christ, then I realize the presence of the Comforter he sent. And lastly I myself appear—his disciple, small and fearful. Only in this perspective can I put my fears in their rightful place.

☙ HEARTBEAT: *When you reach a fearful place in your life today, turn your eyes to the risen Christ. Paint a word picture of what you see.*

2

A CROSS AND A BELL

All this is from God, who reconciled us to himself through Christ and gave us the ministry of reconciliation.

2 Corinthians 5:18 NIV

Not every recollection of Germany is a happy one. Some memories, like a cracked bell and a charred cross that I saw in Lübeck, speak of healing wounds. But these scars tell a remarkable story of reconciliation between two former enemies.

The Marienkirche was a target for bombing in World War II. The Allies scored a direct hit on the church in retaliation against Germany for the destruction of the cathedral in Coventry, England. As the heat of the flames reached the belfry of the church, the metal of the bell expanded in response and it began to toll wildly. The bell's tolling told what was happening. Farm families came from around the countryside to form a bucket brigade to save the rest of the church.

In its death throes, the bell fell from its tower to the floor below. It remains there today, cracked and silent, as its own memorial. After the war, teams of Christians came to Germany from Allied nations to help rebuild the churches that had been destroyed. With them came charred timbers from Coventry Cathedral.

Next to the cracked bell in Marienkirche, charred timbers form a simple cross not unlike a charred cross that stands today in old Coventry Cathedral itself. On the ruined wall behind the cross are simple words that will echo for eternity: "Father forgive."

These symbols of faith are scars that tell a story of reconciliation. They remind me of all the broken relationships in my life, all of my so-called enemies. If that cracked bell and charred cross can live side by side, if Coventry and Lübeck can be reconciled, then surely I can find a way.

☞ HEARTBEAT: *Identify a conflict in your life that seems irreconcilable. Write a prayer of forgiveness that can make the reconciliation possible.*

3

A FORGOTTEN CANDLE

Always be prepared to give an answer to everyone who asks you to give the reason for the hope that you have.

1 Peter 3:15 NIV

Roland and Elke lit a red candle in the living room window on the first Sunday in Advent in 1985. Another glorious Christmas season was about to begin in Germany. "We light this red candle at this time every year," Roland told me, "to look forward to the day when Germany will be reunified, when our people will no longer be divided by the Berlin Wall." Roland continued describing his sadness that so many West Germans had forgotten what this tradition means. "They light the candles every year, but they don't know what it means, and they don't really believe reunification can ever happen."

Four years later the whole world watched by satellite link as the Berlin Wall fell. On the brink of another Advent season, an American news commentator stood at the Wall where candles flickered in the background.

"These candles," asked the anchor in their Atlanta studio, "we see them every night. What do they mean?"

"I don't know," the answer came back from the journalist in Berlin. "It must be a tradition."

How easily we forget the reason for our traditions! People around the world prayed for the Berlin Wall to fall and then were surprised when God answered their prayers. But God had not forgotten.

Today, Germany is politically reunified, but much darkness still exists in that nation and in the rest of this world. I'm lighting a candle as I'm writing to remind me that Jesus Christ is the Light of the world and the Glory of the Father. He alone can bring true peace to troubled regions all across our globe. May we remain diligent in praying for peace until the day the Prince of Peace returns to reign as King of kings and Lord of lords.

☞ HEARTBEAT: *Remember a worthwhile tradition you had forgotten.*

4

A WORK IN PROGRESS

I [Paul] have planted, Apollos watered; but
God gave the increase.

1 Corinthians 3:6 KJV

A little church along the Lahn River in Marburg serves a hot meal on Sundays for less than a dollar. Such a bargain was certain to attract students, as it does each week. One Sunday two young women sat down next to me.

"This is such a friendly church," Renate greeted me. I hadn't even said hello! She had come to town to visit her sister, a medical student. Liesel was going through difficulties in her studies and personal life. Renate had asked her sister if she knew of a good church in Marburg. Although Liesel wasn't a believer, she had heard about the Ufer-Kirche.

I marveled how God had pointed the two sisters to that church that day. I asked if there was any way I could be of assistance. As an American, I didn't have the sense of distance that German professors have with their students. But God planned to use more than me and Renate to reach Liesel. In fact, he had already been at work and not all the pieces were yet in place.

When I invited Liesel to Christus-Treff, I learned that she lived right across the street from the bookstore and knew exactly where I meant! On Thursday night she was the first to arrive. After the service, she spotted a familiar face. "You!" she shrieked at my friend Klaus-Peter. "You're the one who told me about Ufer-Kirche!"

Several years before, Klaus-Peter had spotted a lonely young woman hitchhiking and offered her a ride. When the subject of faith came up, Liesel told him that she wasn't a believer. As he dropped her at her destination, Klaus-Peter said, "If you ever want to talk about it more, come to Ufer-Kirche." The morning of her deep despair when her sister asked her if she knew a good church, Liesel remembered Klaus-Peter's words.

I don't know the end of Liesel's journey of faith. But I am sure that God, who went to so much trouble to show me the lesson of planting and watering, will someday share with us the story of how he gave increase and finished the work that he began through us.

☞ HEARTBEAT: *Recall an example: (1) when you "planted," (2) when you "watered," (3) when you saw God's increase.*

5

A GERMAN ATTIC

Listen to this dream I had.

Genesis 37:6 NIV

Listen to this dream that was one of the last entries in my journal during my last sabbatical year in Marburg:

"The year was coming to an end and it was time to pack up. I was pleased I could fit everything I owned into a few suitcases and small boxes. But then I went downstairs and found a basement full of belongings that I had forgotten about. I discovered things I had brought with me to Germany when my sabbatical began and other things that I had acquired over long years of visiting Germany. I could not nor did I wish to take all of it with me.

"It was time to sort through and pack it all up. What had I brought with me that should be left here for others? And what had I acquired in Germany that was worth packing up and taking back to America?"

At first, I wasn't sure myself what the dream really meant. But in the weeks that followed, friends dropped by the house and gave me clues about the valuable things I was leaving behind.

Werner, a nurse, was grateful for my stories about looking for Jesus in our patients. He had found more time for a difficult old woman since our conversation. Steffi, preparing for elementary education, was glad to hear from a pediatrician that children have a special role in the spiritual formation of adults. Andrea, a teen from a troubled home who came to the English worship service, found hope that middle-aged people can listen to kids and understand.

I had some "American attitudes" that I arrived with that I needed to throw away. I do not automatically know better than anyone else in the world! My encounters with another culture now help me spot when my preferences are not the only or necessarily the best way that things can be accomplished.

Perhaps more important than what I left behind is what I took home to America with me. My struggle with a foreign language helps me understand my patients in the United States who struggle with English.

Nothing in the German attic of my heart that belongs to God will ever get lost.

🍃 HEARTBEAT: *In your prayer time this morning ask God to identify something in the attic of your heart that you should give away, something to throw away, and something to keep.*

_____

_____

_____

_____

_____

_____

_____

11
FEAR NO EVIL

The worst evil of all is to leave the ranks of the living before one dies.

Seneca

1

A SWISS VALLEY

*Yea, though I walk through the valley of the
shadow of death, I will fear no evil.*

Psalm 23:4 KJV

I was in a sunroom off the hospice unit of a Swiss hospital when I saw her. She was sitting in a rocking chair, lovingly fingering the flowers of a Christmas cactus, showing another patient how glorious the blossoms were. Her red-tinted hair fibbed audaciously about her age. Unapologetically she mixed the language of her birth nation with that of her adopted land. This one woman seemed to fill the room with the light of her presence.

I wanted to hear more about the compassionate care of the terminally ill given on this ward. Dr. Noémi came to fetch me, but I was reluctant to give up this moment. "That Italian woman," I said. "She seems to care for the other patients." I wondered what sort of cancer she had, how long she would live.

"Oh, yes," Noémi answered. "I know who you mean. She doesn't have cancer at all. She came here with a broken leg. There were no other beds in the hospital, so she came to us. She's wonderful with the other patients."

How remarkable, I thought. She wasn't afraid to be there. She had no fear of those who would surely die. Instead, she walked with them fearlessly. I remember times when I've been caught off guard in a frightening place where I "didn't belong."

Shortly after language school I developed vertigo and visited a German specialist who didn't speak English. To check my inner ear, he ran hot water into my outer ear and asked me to count backward from one hundred—in German. I felt as if I were trapped in the mind of a two-year-old retarded child. All I could think of was my own powerlessness. I wanted to get out of there as quickly as I could. Then the doctor smiled gently and held my hand.

I often think of this dear woman whose own fearlessness helps others negotiate dark valleys. Her gift of courage in this tiny corner of the world was a testimony to me of the love, hope, and faith that I need to carry into my own world.

☞ HEARTBEAT: *Name a person who walked with you through a dark valley and took away your sense of loneliness.*

2

A JAW BREAKER FOR DEATH

You lifted me out of the depths and did not let my enemies gloat over me.

Psalm 30:1 NIV

I don't know about you, but I've always squirmed a bit when I've tried to apply the psalmist's thoughts about his enemies to my own life. For example, I can't think of anyone whose teeth I would like God to break by striking them on the jaw (Psalm 3:7). (Well, maybe I can think of someone, but I will refrain from offering the prayer!)

I used to pass those verses by until I visited a friend who was in the hospital for cancer surgery. I found LaRee smiling at the Psalms one morning. "Look at the promise God gave me!" she said, pointing to Psalm 94. LaRee had rewritten the words this way: "Who rises up for LaRee against the wicked tumor? Who stands up for LaRee against the evil cells? The Lord our God will wipe them out."

My friend found an effective way to pray for her own healing in verses I had ignored. After that visit, I went through my Bible and found every time David used the words *enemy* or *foe*. I thought about friends on my prayer list and came up with these power prayers:

"You exalted Jen above the breast cancer; from violent effects of chemotherapy you rescued her" (Psalm 18:48).

"When lupus advances against Jill to devour her kidneys, when her lymphocytes attack her, they will stumble and fall" (Psalm 27:2).

"Carl's arthritis will be ashamed and dismayed; it will turn back in sudden disgrace" (Psalm 6:10).

"How long must Nancy wrestle with her thoughts and every day have sorrow in her heart? How long will the Alzheimer's triumph over her?" (Psalm 13:2).

I'm sure you can personalize these verses as well. If you find yourself smiling at some of these power prayers, you've learned something new about prayer. As LaRee pointed out to me in Psalm 94:19: "When the cares of my heart are many, your consolations cheer my soul."

> ☞ HEARTBEAT: *Name something you fear. Instead of the word enemy, place that fear in three of these psalms as a personal prayer.*

_____

_____

_____

_____

_____

_____

_____

_____

_____

_____

3

A PRAYER SOUP RECIPE

The eyes of all look to you, and you give them their food at the proper time.

Psalm 145:15 NIV

Jane knew she was in for a tough time when she crossed over the yellow line on the hospital floor into a "life island." Under the best of circumstances, a bone marrow transplantation is a difficult ordeal. Jane was prepared for the radiation and heavy chemo, and she was even ready to stay in this small isolation room. But it never occurred to her that she would be taken to the limits of endurance by a microwaved mound of mystery meat that lay like a lump on the sterile plate before her. What appetite she had quickly disappeared.

Rescue came in the person of a friend. This godsend named Ginny chatted with the nutritionist, then headed for home with large bottles of sterile water and a foolproof recipe for Jane's relief. She returned the next day with a grin on her face and large containers of "prayer soup." Within minutes, a warmed-up sample had the nurses' noses twitching in interest and the doctors' stomachs rumbling a respectful salute.

With Ginny's help, Jane was able to eat enough on her own to support her weight. Her amazing appetite was credited to the "prayer soup." The basic soup ingredients grew out of the nutritionist's list, but, as you probably guessed, there was a special "secret" ingredient. Each

day Ginny used alphabet noodle letters to spell out a prayer for Jane—
and then threw them into the pot.

Five years later, the staff fondly remembers those daily visits to
Jane. They knew Ginny was going through treatment for cancer herself at the time. Equally fondly, they remember the recipe for "prayer
soup" and offer invisible noodles of their own from time to time as
secret ingredients in their patient care.

🎿 HEARTBEAT: *Write your own recipe for a "prayer
soup."*

4

A FUTURE WITH HOPE

"For I know the plans I have for you," declares the LORD, "plans to prosper you and not to harm you, plans to give you hope and a future."
Jeremiah 29:11 NIV

I told you earlier about Crumb Bunny and her bone marrow donor. The child was only two months old when I was called in on her case and seventeen months old when she entered a "life island" a few doors down from Jane. She had the best that modern medicine could offer and Chrissie's donated marrow, but that was not enough.

One day I stopped by a bookstore in search of words of hope. In the window hung a small watercolor painting with Jeremiah's verse about a hopeful future. A clever little bird seemed to add his own *amen* to the design. I stared at the painting and debated whether to buy it. Was this God's personal message for Crumb Bunny? Her future was anything but secure if we measured it in terms of medical certainties. What would this verse mean to her young parents—a holy promise or a cruel hoax?

Going with my instincts and love for their baby, I bought the little painting and brought it to the Bone Marrow Unit. "Oh!" exclaimed her mom. "I was just reading that verse yesterday myself and kept wondering what God meant about it for Katherine." Sue hung it prominently on the bulletin board just outside her daughter's laminar air-flow room. It remained there until Crumb Bunny's discharge.

Sixteen months later I stood in Crumb Bunny's bedroom at home watching the now healthy child sleep. My little gift was prominently displayed above her bed. And hanging next door in the guest room was another gift from a friend—a little stained-glass piece using the same Bible verse. Not knowing about my gift or that Sue had claimed this Scripture promise for her daughter, another friend had acted on her instincts. God took no chances in letting Crumb Bunny—and us—know his special plans for her future.

☞ HEARTBEAT: *Is there a Bible verse that came to you from many different sources within a short period of time? How has that verse affected your life?*

5

A LOWLY ASSOCIATION

*Live in harmony with one another; do not be
haughty, but associate with the lowly.*
Romans 12:16 RSV

My dog Jenny lived a long, happy life. Her death left me looking
for the next furry version of perfect, which I found in a two-year-old,
pre-owned Yorkie named Ashley, who came into my home with his
head hung low.

All my neighbors were waiting for me to come home from the
Humane Society with the newest member of my family. In the presence
of men, Ashley would shake like a leaf. That was when I realized that
this little dog was terrified of men. The first time I picked up a newspaper
and saw him cower, Ashley's past history started to unfold.

All my male friends are gentle, but their imposing sizes and
booming voices seemed to terrorize the little guy. I wanted all my
friends to be a part of Ashley's life. There had to be a way for Ashley
to be healed of his fear.

Whenever a man came to the door, I picked up Ashley and held
him in my arms. Then my visitor would gently stroke the dog's head
and talk to him in a soothing voice. When Ashley relaxed, I would
hand him into male arms to be held and petted for a few more minutes.

After some weeks, Ashley remembered each man he met this
way. He stopped cowering and shaking. In fact, after meeting my next-

door neighbor Bob, Ashley stole into his house. The dog reappeared a few minutes later to drop one of Bob's dirty socks at his feet. Bob, he seemed to be saying, was more than safe. Bob was accepted.

By coming into my family, Ashley was healed of his fear and could live at peace with all men. "Love the animals," said Dostoyevsky. "God has given them the rudiments of thought and joy untroubled. Don't trouble it, don't harass them, don't deprive them of their happiness, don't work against God's intent." How blessed our lives can be when we work with and within God's intent.

☞ HEARTBEAT: *Name some abused creature you know—human or animal—who could use some creative healing. What can you do to catalyze that healing?*

12
WEEDS INTO WILDFLOWERS

I found a phrase in every phase of yesterday.

Burl Ives

1

LOVE THAT MATTERS

Is anyone among you suffering?

James 5:13 RSV

There's an elderly man in my church who takes my hand every Sunday, either entering church or leaving, and whispers, "I love you." I know exactly what he means.

He and his bride of sixty seasons still live in their own home (by the grace of God). Every year they get a bit frailer, but they never miss a Sunday at church. Last year Emma had a frightening year, bad enough to frighten Lou. That was the Sunday he began to whisper in my ear.

"I'm afraid that Emma has Alzheimer's." She stood by his side with her sweet smile. I didn't know whether she heard us or not. There were tears in his eyes. "I don't know what to do," Lou confessed. He loved his bride too much to err.

By the grace of God, we have a wonderful geriatric clinic at my hospital. I've seen my friends, adult children, come away relieved. Their elderly parents find peace as well. I gave Lou the information. The next Sunday he had tears in his eyes again. "Thank you so much," he whispered. "It was just old age, not Alzheimer's. I don't know how to thank you." Four years later, he and Emma still live on their own at home.

That was when Lou initiated his liturgy. Each Sunday he murmurs in my ear, "I love you." Each week he reminds me that God offers a comprehensive health care package to those he loves. We are all caregivers in a system—Christ's church—that provides endless benefits for those who share the love of God.

> ❦ HEARTBEAT: *Think of someone who has helped you. Plan a surprising time and place to say "I love you."*

2

MONSIEUR AND MIDGE

*So go on cheering and strengthening each
other, as I have no doubt you are doing.*
1 Thessalonians 5:11 JBP

I was visiting friends one night for dinner and noticed that their
big old Labrador retriever and their young toy poodle were inseparable.
I thought it was sweet of the old dog to tolerate the fresh little newcomer
into his home. But their relationship was deeper than I had imagined.

As they walked from the kitchen to the living room, Midge (the
Lab) was always following Monsieur (the poodle). They always
seemed close enough to touch. As I looked at Midge's venerable old
eyes, I saw that they were clouded with cataracts. She was blind—
and Monsieur was her Seeing Eye dog!

My friends explained how the two dogs formed their relationship. It was the dogs' own idea. Monsieur stifled all his puppy antics
for the sake of his old sister. My friends had come to love Monsieur
all the more because of his loving concern for their old Midge.

That incident occurred more than twenty years ago, but the
image of the two dogs has never left my heart. Midge and Monsieur
come back every time I feel someone threatening to change my neat
little world. There have been times I felt like a fresh little poodle,
wanting to move at my own pace and not let anyone slow me down.
But at other times I feel like a tired old dog needing help. We are

here in this world to share our gifts, to know when to give and when to receive.

   🐝 HEARTBEAT: *Recall a time when you felt like a tired, old dog when someone younger and livelier strengthened and cheered you.*

3

MALEDIZIÓNE
TO BENEDIZIÓNE

Our God turned the curse into a blessing.
Nehemiah 13:2 KJV

One of the extraordinary events on a trip to Italy was a guest spot on a national TV show. Italian parents of children with cancer wanted me to tell their countrymen about a worldwide effort known as "Candlelighters." As the name and motto suggest, the parents who belong to this organization would rather "light one candle than curse the darkness."

The mamas and papas had written out their questions for the host, who would pose the questions in Italian and pretend he understood my answers in English. "Just make sure I know which order they're going to be asked in!" I begged. (Gianni and Bruno had fallen into a spirited argument over whose question would come first.)

After the taping, the man who was to dub in over my English listened for any words he didn't understand. "There's one word I don't know how to translate," he told me. The word was *curse*. None of the fifteen Italians gathered there could help. Suddenly, I had a flash of recollection and cried out, "I know! *Maledizióne!*"

Of all the words I might know in Italian, how did I know *maledizióne*? Anyone with a passion for opera could tell you. In this case, it was *La Forza del Destino* that brought it to mind. In Verdi's tragic melodrama, Leonora's ill-fated romance left a trail of blood and many *maledizióne*.

There is a sequel to this adventure. Sometime later, I returned to Italy. When I detrained in Milan, the conductor startled me by planting a kiss on both my cheeks and uttering a single word: *Benedizióne*. Blessing.

I learned that he was the father of a child with leukemia who recognized me from the TV appearance. By joining other "Candlelighters," he spreads hope and blessing to other children with cancer and to their loved ones.

This man taught me a remarkable lesson. The world would expect someone like him to have a curse on his lips. But instead he spoke a blessing.

One by one we can make a difference in this world. We can be a blessing, too.

Benedizióne, dear friend.

☙ HEARTBEAT: *Name someone who turned a curse into a blessing for you.*

4

THE FAITHFUL HEADACHE

What you have heard from me through many witnesses entrust to faithful people who will be able to teach others as well.

2 Timothy 2:2 NRSV

When I was in college, I taught Sunday school at a residential institution for epileptics in New York State. My class at Craig Colony had the lowest IQs and the most seizures. The first Sunday I taught, one of my students fell on the floor in a "fit." I was seventeen years old and in shock.

"That's okay, dear," one of my other students comforted me. "We'll take care of this. You just keep on preaching." And I did, for four long years.

As you can imagine, my youth and inexperience made this difficult situation even harder. Every Sunday I went home with a headache, but I never told anyone. I often questioned just what I was accomplishing. Did my students understand anything I said? But I went on faithfully for the entire time I was in college.

In later years, I rarely thought about Craig Colony and never thought about my doubts. Places like Craig closed many years ago in favor of bringing the people closer to their families. Thirty years later on a Sunday afternoon, I visited a regional center for the developmentally disabled in the same area of New York State.

The chaplain invited me to their worship service. There I met a short, rotund, retarded man who kept smiling at me. Strange! Finally I asked him, "Do you think you know me?" He nodded energetically. How could he possibly know me? I had never been there before. "Craig Colony," was his reply. "I was at Craig."

It was not my words as much as my faithfulness that had told that little man about Jesus. Mother Teresa said that God does not call us to be successful—simply faithful. But God is kind enough to give us a clue, every thirty years or so, that our headaches and our faithfulness are not in vain.

☞ HEARTBEAT: *Make a record of some small act of faithfulness on your part today. Imagine how God may share the follow-up with you in the future.*

5

WEEDS INTO WILDFLOWERS

Therefore we will not fear though the earth
should change, though the mountains shake
in the heart of the sea.

Psalm 46:2 RSV

There has never been a time in my life with so many major changes. The greenhouse where I used to grow orchids came down to make way for a new garage. First the orchids died in a freeze, then the friend who introduced me to orchids died himself. It was time for a change, so I earn my green equity outdoors these days, sorting weeds from wildflowers.

Babu tries to help me in the garden but gets into every stickle burr on the acre. He's only a baby and doesn't yet know how to care for his Yorkie coiffure. This half-pint pup came into my life because my beloved Ashley passed on in January. Two months of Yorkie-free life was about all I could handle, so I'm back training another little terrierist.

Last year I reduced my activities at Yale to make more time to write about the things that God is doing in my life. Gratefully, this gives me time to get back to Marburg several times a year now, whether it's a sabbatical year or not. My last trip to Germany I started to reread Luke's gospel. When my adventure back to faith began with Dr. Luke's carefully written accounts, I never dreamed that Luke and I would have so much in common, combining medicine and ministry.

Perhaps the greatest change of all was going back to Ohio with my sister and nephews to bury our dad. There was no home to go home to. We drove past the vacant house where a lonely ladder stood in the empty living room as if the new owners hardly knew where to begin with the fixin' up. We were grateful for the refuge of a Residence Inn with its homey fireplace during those days we said good-bye. Only a miracle of grace could transform something as mundane as a motel room into a haven of rest.

In this season of life with so many changes, I haven't been afraid. It's as if each step was ordered and planned and linked to the next. I wonder what weeds God will bring to me next year that need to be transformed into wildflowers?

🌱 HEARTBEAT: *Name some change in your life that you fear. Imagine how God might work that out for your good.*

_____

_____

_____

_____

_____

_____

_____

SOME EXTRA SYSTOLES

Scott Bolinder and Lyn Cryderman have partnered me through five books as my publisher and editor. These dear friends will doubtless recognize some of their own cooking in a bite or two of *Breakfast*. This book was Lori Walburg's first chance to find out what a Faithful Headache I can be. My thanks to each of them and the entire Zondervan team.

My deepest thanks go to my German partners in ministry, Elke and Roland Werner, and all the other Christus-Trefflers who are my brothers and sisters in my "home away from home."